Editorial Manager
Elizabeth Morris, Ph. D.

Editor-in-Chief
Sharon Coan, M.S. Ed.

Cover Artist
Lesley Palmer

Art Coordinator
Kevin Barnes

Art Director
CJae Froshay

Imaging
Alfred Lau
Ralph Olmedo, Jr.

Product Manager
Phil Garcia

Acknowledgements

Microsoft® Office Software is
©1991–2002 Microsoft Corporation.
All Rights Reserved. *Microsoft® Office*
is a trademark of Microsoft Corporation,
registered in the U. S. and other
countries. Microsoft Clip Art ©2002.
All rights reserved.

Publishers
Rachelle Cracchiolo, M.S. Ed.
Mary Dupuy Smith, M.S. Ed.

Creative Projects Using Templates for Microsoft Office™

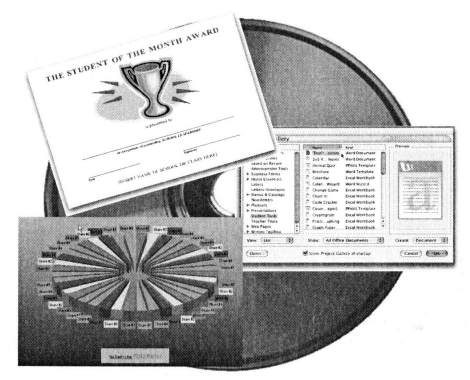

Authors

Sara Connolly
Lynn Van Gorp, M.S.

Teacher Created Materials, Inc.
6421 Industry Way
Westminster, CA 92683
www.teachercreated.com.

ISBN-0-7439-3876-3
©2003 Teacher Created Materials, Inc.
Reprinted, 2004
Made in U.S.A.

Table of Contents

Table of Contents *(cont.)*

Introduction

About This Book

With *Creative Projects Using Templates for Microsoft Office™*, you can use over 75 *Microsoft Word*, *Excel*, and *PowerPoint* templates to simplify your classroom tasks and turn student assignments into dazzling presentations.

The templates included with this book are files that have already been created for you to use in completing the tasks or exercises that you frequently perform throughout the school year. They save you time because you do not need to "start from scratch" with every form, recording sheet, or certificate. Templates can be used again and again, and are easily modified for various occasions.

Administrators and teachers will find forms ranging from medication dispensing to instructions for substitute teachers, permissions slips, grade books, recognition awards, and much more.

Students can turn an animal report into an interactive quiz, remember weekly spelling words with a game of hangman, and answer a few simple questions to create a newsletter. They can also learn more about taking notes, organize their school schedules, and use a checklist to improve their writing. Many of the terrific templates provided on the enclosed CD can be printed in color, black and white, or grayscale.

This book provides step-by-step instructions for how to enter the unique information appropriate for any particular use. There are also many extension ideas for exciting new ways that you may have never thought of before to use these templates!

Using the Templates

The templates provided on the CD-ROM can either be accessed directly from the CD or copied to your computer's hard drive. If you choose to access them directly from the CD, open the *Microsoft Office* application required by the template. (See the Index on pages 171–174 for a list of the templates and required applications.) Go to the **File** menu and select **Open**. Navigate to the CD-ROM and open either the **Teacher Tools** folder or the **Student Tools** folder. Double-click the template file to open it.

If you have the space available on your computer (about 185 MB of hard disk space is needed), it is recommended that you copy the templates into your *Microsoft Office* program files. Open your *Microsoft Office* program folder and open the **Templates** folder. Copy the **Student Tools** and **Teacher Tools** folders into the **Templates** folder.

If you are using *Microsoft Office 97, 98,* or *2000,* you can go to the **File** Menu, select **New**, and then choose the **Student Tools** or **Teacher Tools** tabs on the New Document dialog box to access the templates.

If you are using *Microsoft Office XP*, you can select the templates from the **Template Gallery**. If you are using *Microsoft Office 2001* or *X*, you can select the templates from the **Project Gallery**.

See the Template Tips and Tricks section on pages 169–170 for more information on using templates.

About The Templates

These templates were developed by Microsoft's Education Division for use with *Microsoft Office* applications. For more information on Microsoft's Education division, visit their website at

http://www.microsoft.com/education/tl

Introduction *(cont.)*

System Requirements

For PCs with Microsoft Windows:
The specific hardware requirements for *Office* will vary based on your operating system. Listed below are suggested minimum requirements:

- Personal computer with a Pentium 133 MHz or higher processor
- 32 MB of memory (RAM)
- CD-ROM drive
- VGA or higher-resolution monitor; Super VGA recommended
- *Microsoft Office 97* or any combination of *97* or higher versions of *Microsoft Word, Microsoft Excel,* and *Microsoft PowerPoint*
  Office 2000 requires Windows 95 and higher. *Office XP* requires Windows 98 and higher, or Windows NT with Service Pack 6

For Macintosh Computers
- Any PowerPC-based (or higher) Mac-OS-compatible system; System 7.5 or later
- 16 MB of memory (RAM)
- CD-ROM drive
- Color monitor
- *Microsoft Office 98* or any combination of *98* or higher versions of *Microsoft Word, Microsoft Excel,* or *Microsoft PowerPoint*

Macro Information

Many of the Teacher Tools or Student Tools templates have macros included in them. A macro is a set of computer instructions used to automate tasks in *Microsoft Office* programs. Some computer viruses have been found in macros, which is the reason that *Office* has a built-in Macro Virus Protection feature. This feature can be turned off or on in the **Options** (Windows) or **Preferences** (Macintosh) menu.

If you have Macro Virus Protection turned on and you open a template that contains macros, you will be notified with a warning dialog box. Since these templates are from a trusted source, click **Enable Macros**. If you disable macros, some of the features of a template, or an entire template, may not work correctly.

About The Version of *Microsoft Office* Used in this Book

The screenshots in this book were taken from *Microsoft Office 2000* for Windows and *Microsoft Office X* for Macintosh. Though many of the menus and dialog boxes may have a different appearance, the content will be the same. When necessary, instructions are provided for older versions of *Microsoft Office.*

"Don't Miss It!" Posters

Software Application

Microsoft Word

Using the Template

1. "Don't Miss It!" posters are perfect for your class events or fundraisers. There are five posters available in the template—Get on Target, Parent-Teacher Night, Yard Sale, Book Sale, and Annual Car Wash. Scroll down to view all the templates.

2. To personalize the "Don't Miss It—Get on Target" template by adding the date and location of your event, click inside the text box at the right-hand side of the document. Select the word "date" and the symbols around it. Type the date of your event.

3. To personalize the remaining templates, click inside the textbox that appears under the graphic. Select the **Insert School Name Here** text. Type the name of your school. Then click the lines underneath and type the location and time of the event. You may have to change the font size, color, or style to make it more suitable for the poster.

4. If possible, print the poster in color.

"Don't Miss It" Posters *(cont.)*

Modifying the Template

- You can modify this template for another kind of event. For example, you could modify the Car Wash template to create an Open House poster.

To change the picture, click the existing picture and press the delete button. To add a new picture, go to the **Insert** menu and select **Picture**. If you would like to add a new picture from the Microsoft Clip Gallery, select **Clip Art…**. Resize the picture so that it fits in the space provided.

All you need to do now is replace the words "Annual Car Wash" with "Open House." Change "Location" to "Date," add the time, and your poster is ready to print.

Tips and Tricks

- If you have trouble moving the picture, you may need to format it differently. Click the picture to select it. Go to the **Format** menu and select **Picture**. If you are using *Word 97* or *98*, go to the **Position** tab and select **Float Over Text**. (This isn't necessary for subsequent versions of *Word*.) Then you can select how you would like the text to wrap around the picture.

Brochure

Application

Microsoft Word

Using the Template

1. You can begin customizing the Brochure template by typing your school name and the title of your brochure in the upper right corner above the school house.

2. Scroll down to the second page. This is where you will be adding most of the text for your brochure. The text that is already on the page has directions for creating your brochure. You might want to print this page to use as a reference as you work on your brochure.

3. Each column on this page has a text box. To replace the text, first click inside the box. Then you can simply type over the existing text. If you want to remove the existing text before typing, go to the **Edit** menu and select **Clear** and then **Contents**.

Brochure *(cont.)*

Modifying the Template

- You could modify the template to make it specific to a subject or school activity. For example, you could create a brochure about the school science fair.

  Start by replacing the graphic. Select the existing graphic and press the backspace or delete key. Then go to the **Insert** menu and select **Picture**. If you want to use the Microsoft Clip Gallery, select **Clip Art**. If you want to use a graphic from your files, select **From File**.

  If you are using the Microsoft Clip Gallery, you can either scroll through the categories or type the words you are looking for into the **Search:** box. (In the example below, the graphic was found in the **Science and Technology** category.)

  Select the graphic you wish to add and click **Insert**.

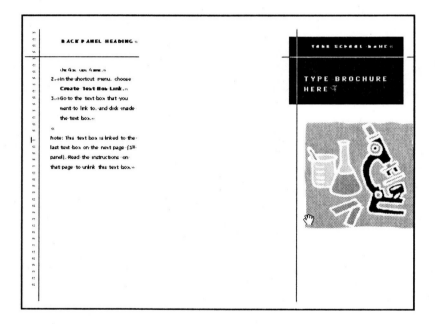

  If you have trouble making the graphic and text appear the way that you want them, you may need to change the way that the text wraps around the graphic. Select the graphic and then click the **Format** menu. Select **Picture**. If you are using *Microsoft Word* 97 or 98, go to the **Position** tab and select **Float Over Text**. (This isn't necessary for subsequent versions of *Word*.) Then you can select how you would like the text to wrap around the picture. In this instance, you might want to select **In Front of Text** as the Wrapping Style.

Tips and Tricks

- The instructions that appear on the brochure include information on how to unlink a text box by right-clicking on the text box itself and then selecting **Break Forward Link** from the Shortcut menu. If you are using a Macintosh computer, you can make the same Shortcut menu appear by holding down the **Control** key as you click the text box.

Calendar

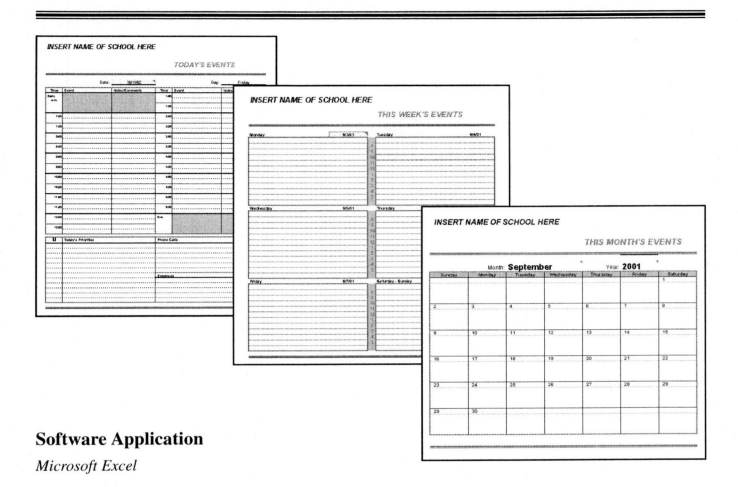

Software Application

Microsoft Excel

Using the Template

1. The Calendar template includes a calendar for monthly events, weekly events, and today's events. To select a type of calendar, click its tab at the bottom of the worksheet.

2. The red arrows in the template indicate that comments are attached. The comments provide additional tips for creating your calendar. To view a comment, hold your mouse over the cell until the comment appears.

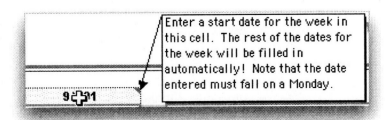

Calendar *(cont.)*

3. When you add start dates to the calendar, *Excel* will automatically fill in the day of the week for the Daily calendar or the remaining dates for the week for the Weekly calendar. When you add the month and year for the Monthly calendar, *Excel* will automatically fill in the days of the month accordingly. If you make any changes to the template, *Excel* will adjust the template accordingly.

Tips and Tricks

- When you open the worksheet, you may get a warning about Macros in the document. Select **Enable Macros**. If you disable the macros, the worksheet will not work correctly.

- If you have more than one event that you want to list within a cell on the monthly calendar, you can enter a hard return to separate the text without moving to a new cell.

  If you are using a Windows computer, hold down the **Alt** key as you press **Enter**. If you are using a Macintosh computer, hold down the **command** key and the **option** key as you press **return**.

Calendar Wizard

Software Application

Microsoft Word

Using the Template

1. The Calendar Wizard takes you through a step-by step process to personalize your calendar. When you see the Start screen, press **Next** to continue.

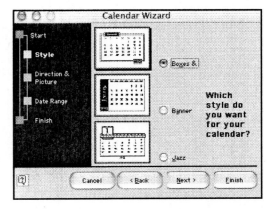

2. Decide which kind of style you want for your calendar. If you are going to be adding information into your calendar, you might want to select the boxes style. If your calendar is intended as a reference or a more decorative purpose, you might want to select the banner or jazz style. Click **Next** to continue.

Calendar Wizard *(cont.)*

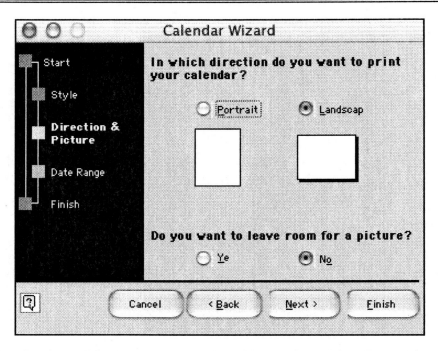

3. Select the direction in which you want your calendar to print, either *Portrait* (vertical) or *Landscape* (horizontal). Then decide if you want to leave room for a picture. Depending on the style and direction you have selected, you might find a picture takes up too much room. Click **Next** to continue.

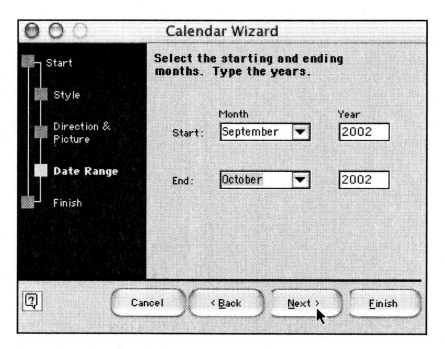

4. Select the starting and ending date of your calendar. Make sure that you enter the years in the boxes provided. Click **Next** to continue.

Calendar Wizard *(cont.)*

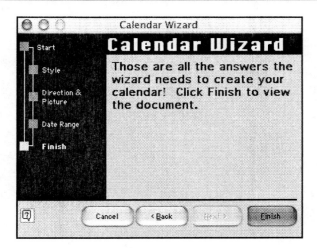

5. Your calendar is ready for you to view! Click **Finish** to exit the Wizard and see your personalized calendar.

6. If there is anything you want to change about your calendar, or if you want to use a different style than the one you chose, simply open the Calendar Wizard and start again.

Modifying the Template

- You can change the graphic that the template automatically adds to the calendar and replace it with a graphic that is specific to a season or holiday, or even a graphic that represents your school. To do this, make sure that you chose the option to leave room for a picture in Step 3. If you did not, open the Calendar Wizard again and start over.

  Click the existing picture. Then go to the **Insert** menu and select **Picture**. If you want to use the Microsoft Clip Gallery, select **Clip Art**. If you want to use a graphic that you have in your files, select **From File**.

  If you are using the Clip Gallery, scroll through the categories to find an appropriate graphic. Click the selected graphic and click **Insert**.

  Your new graphic will appear in the space provided by the calendar.

Class Welcome

Software Application

Microsoft PowerPoint

Using the Template

1. The Class Welcome template is a *PowerPoint* presentation that you can customize to welcome parents and students to a new school year. You can enter your own text to inform them about your classroom policies, grading, and goals for the new year.

2. You can customize the template in two ways, either using Outline view or Normal view. Select the existing text and type the text that you want to add.

3. If you have too much information for one slide, you may need to add an additional slide within the presentation. For example you may need two slides for your Mission Statement and Goals section of the presentation. The simplest method of adding a slide is to go to the **Insert** menu and select **Duplicate Slide**.

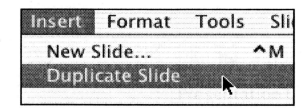

Class Welcome *(cont.)*

4. You can see in Outline view (and Normal view, if you are using *Microsoft PowerPoint 2000* or above), that the duplicate slide has been added to your presentation.

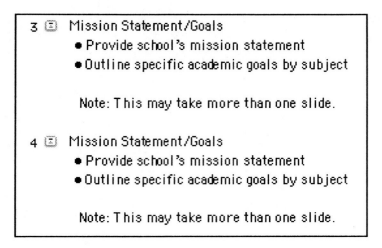

5. If you want to delete a slide from the presentation, select the slide either in Outline view or in Slide Sorter view.

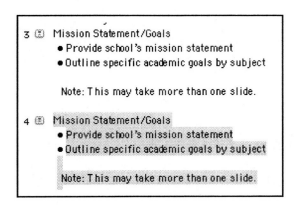
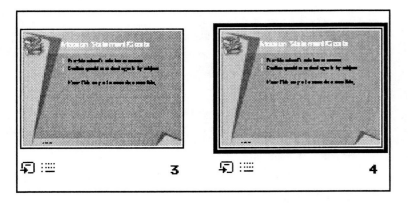

6. Press the backspace or delete key. If you get a message that this action will delete a slide and its contents, click **OK**.

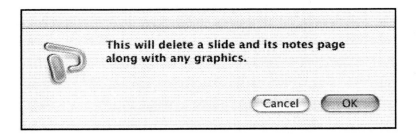

Tips and Tricks

- If you want to change the background of a slide, or add additional eye-catching effects, go to the **Format** menu and select **Slide Background**. You can change the colors or add fill effects.

Field Trip Permission

Insert Name of School Here

FIELD TRIP PERMISSION FORM

Your child's class will be attending a field trip to:

Date:	
Time:	
Location:	

Cost:	
Transportation:	
Notes:	

Please return this permission slip by:

I give permission for my child, _____, in room

_____, to attend the field trip to _____

on _____ from _____ to_____.

Enclosed is $ _____ to cover the cost of the trip. (Exact cash or check made payable to the school.)

In case of an emergency, I give permission for my child to receive medical treatment. In case of such an emergency, please contact:

(Name)	*(Phone Number)*
(Parent/Guardian Signature)	*(Date)*

Software Application

Microsoft Word

Using the Template

1. The next time your class has a field trip planned, use this template to quickly create a permission form to copy and distribute to parents and guardians.

2. Much of the text in the top portion of the template has been formatted in tables. To enter information, click in the first table and type the field trip destination. Click in the second table and type the date, time, and location of your field trip.

Your child's class will be attending a field trip to: The Aquarium of the Pacific	
Date:	September 27, 2002
Time:	10:00 AM to 1:30 PM
Location:	100 Aquarium Way

Field Trip Permission *(cont.)*

3. If you want to change the alignment of the text, select it and then change the alignment using the toolbar or the **Format—Paragraph** menu.

4. Click in the remaining tables and fill in the pertinent information.

Modifying the Template

- To make the template better reflect your field trip's theme, you can change the picture. Select the existing picture and press the backspace or delete key.

  To add a picture from the Clip Art Gallery, go to the **Insert** menu and select **Picture→Clip Art**. Scroll through the different categories until you find the picture that best suits your theme. Select the picture and click **Insert**.

  To add a picture from your files, go to the Insert menu and select **Picture→From File**. Locate your picture and click **Insert**.

  Once your graphic appears on the template, you may need to resize it to fit the available space. Select the graphic (if it is not already selected) and use the lower right-hand grabber handle to resize it.

Your child's class will be attending a field trip to: The Aquarium of the Pacific

Date:	September 27, 2002
Time:	10:00 AM to 1:30 PM
Location:	100 Aquarium Way
Cost:	$8.00 per student
Transportation:	School Bus
Notes:	Lunch will be provided.

Fractions Graphing

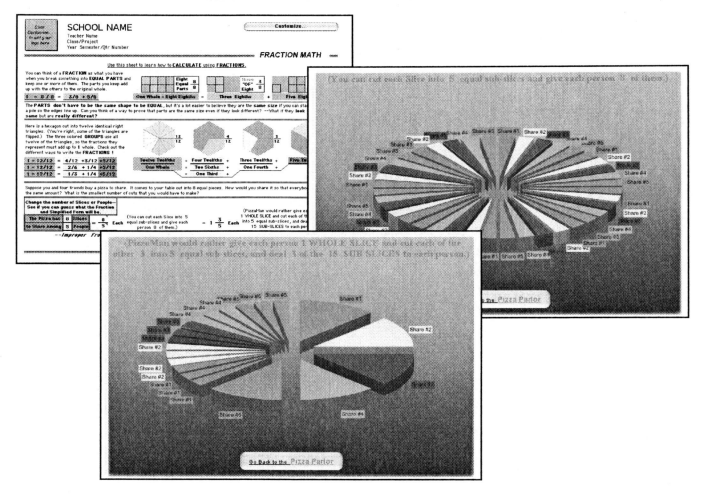

Software Application

Microsoft Excel

Using the Template

1. The Fractions Graphing template can provide students with some basic information about fractions, as well as a graphic representation of a fraction. Press the **Customize** button at the upper right-hand side of the template to customize the template.

2. The small red arrows that you see on the template indicate that there are comments attached. Move your mouse over the red arrow to read the comment.

3. In the "Type School Information Here" section, type your school name, teacher name, class and project, year, and semester or quarter number. You can leave any of these cells blank if the information does not apply.

4. After you've made your changes to this section, notice that the section below also shows this information. This section shows how the text will look in the document. Click the **Change Font** button to change the font of the text.

Fractions Graphing *(cont.)*

5. You can also select a picture to use as a logo for your school or class. Click the **Select Logo** button and select a picture file to use. *Excel* will automatically format it in the space provided.

6. Once you have made the changes, click the **Lock this Sheet** button to save the changes. If you save the changes as part of your template, the logo and school information will appear every time you open the template.

7. To go back to the worksheet and see your changes, click the **Eq. Squares** tab at the bottom of the worksheet.

8. Have students read the top part of the template to learn more about how to use fractions to calculate. Towards the bottom of the page students can try an activity to graph fractions.

9. Have them look first at the example provided. In the example, a pizza has eight slices to be divided among five people. If students place the mouse over the red comment indicators, they will see that the top number in the fraction is the numerator and the bottom is the denominator, along with an explanation of an improper fraction.

10. The first example shows the division of the pizza if each slice is to be divided into five separate sections. The second, "The Easy Way," shows a simplified form in which each person receives one whole slice while the remaining three slices are divided into 15 additional sub-slices.

11. Students can enter new numbers into the worksheet to see how the fractions could be graphed.

Fundraising

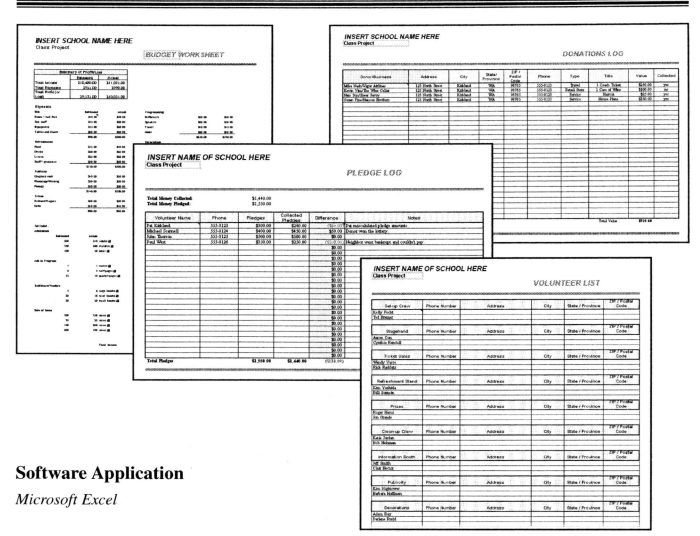

Software Application

Microsoft Excel

Using the Template

The Fundraising template calculates a budget and the estimated and actual profits and losses. It has four separate worksheets—Donations Log, Pledge Log, Volunteer List, and Budget Worksheet. Each of the worksheets has sample information entered into it. The red arrows in the cells indicate that there are comments attached, in this case to provide additional help for using the template. Move your mouse over the red arrow to read the comment.

1. Highlight the **Insert Name of School Here** text at the top of the document. Replace it with the name of your school.

2. To customize the worksheets and add your own data, highlight the sample information and select **Edit➔Clear➔Contents**.

3. Type your own information. *Excel* will make calculations automatically wherever necessary.

4. You can edit any of the cell headers to make them more applicable to your project.

Fundraising *(cont.)*

Tips and Tricks

- When you open the worksheet, you may get a warning about Macros in the document. Select **Enable Macros**. If you disable the macros, the worksheet will not work correctly.

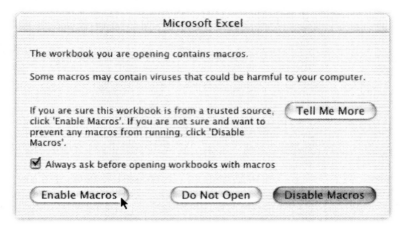

- The names of the expenses in the Budget Worksheet are protected and read-only. If you need to modify these, go to the **Tools** menu, select **Protection**, and select **Unprotect Sheet**. After you have made your changes, you can select **Protect Sheet** from the same menu so that your text cannot be changed.

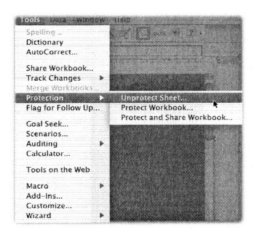

- If the worksheets open at a size on your screen that is too small for you to read, select a new percentage view from the Zoom menu. This will not affect any of the fonts or how the document will look when printed.

Gradebook

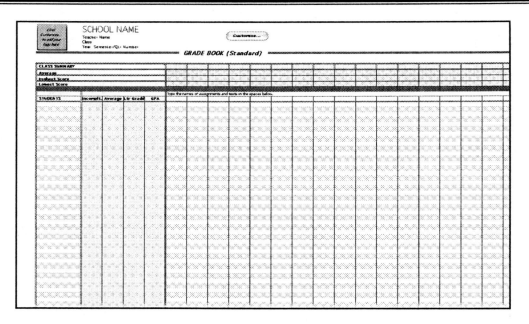

Software Application

Microsoft Excel

Using the Template

1. You can customize the template with your own school information, logos, and grading system. To begin, click the **Customize** button at the top of the worksheet.

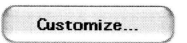

2. The red arrows indicate that comments have been added to a cell. In this instance, they provide valuable tips for using the worksheet. Move your mouse over an arrow to read the comment.

3. Type your school information into the first part of the sheet. Look at the bottom section to see how it will appear in the document. You can leave any of the headers blank and they will not show up in the document.

4. The second section of the sheet is the Grade and GPA table, which indicates the value used for calculating grades. If you want to change any of the values, this is the place to do it. Any changes you make here will be reflected in the gradebook itself.

Gradebook *(cont.)*

5. If you want to use a logo for your gradebook, click **Select Logo**. Find the picture file that you want to use and click **Insert**. *Excel* will automatically fit it into the space provided.

6. To change the font size, style, or color, click the **Change Font** button. Make your selections from the dialog box and click **OK**.

7. When you are satisfied with your changes, click the **Lock/Save Sheet** button. This will save your changes and customize your template so that every time the template is opened, the information will be intact. The button changes to an **Unlock this Sheet** button. If you want to make changes at another time, you will have to select this button first.

8. To return to the gradebook, click the **Standard** tab if you want to use a gradebook for both assignments and tests. Click the **Modified** tab if you want to use a gradebook for just assignments.

Using the Gradebook

1. Type the names of your students in the column labeled "Students."

2. The section beside this column, which is labeled in green, consists of formulas that *Excel* uses to calculate the grades. They are protected and cannot be changed.

3. Type the names of tests and assignments in the row provided.

4. Enter the grades the students achieved on the tests and assignments in the rows labeled with their names. *Excel* automatically calculates the average, letter grade, and GPA for each student, along with the class-wide average, highest score, and lowest score for each assignment and test. These calculations are made according to the grade and GPA table in the Customize section. If any cells in a student's row are left blank, *Excel* will include this in the Incomplete column.

Incomplt.	Average	Ltr Grade	GPA	Test 1	Test 2	Test 3	Test 4	Test 5	
	90%	A-	3.67	90.00	95.00	97.00	86.00	84.00	
	79%	C+	2.33	75.00	55.00	84.00	90.00	91.00	
1	83%	B-	2.67		84.00	75.00	85.00	87.00	

Tips and Tricks

- When you open the worksheet, you may get a warning about Macros in the document. Select **Enable Macros**. If you disable the macros, the worksheet will not work correctly.

Grant Request Letter

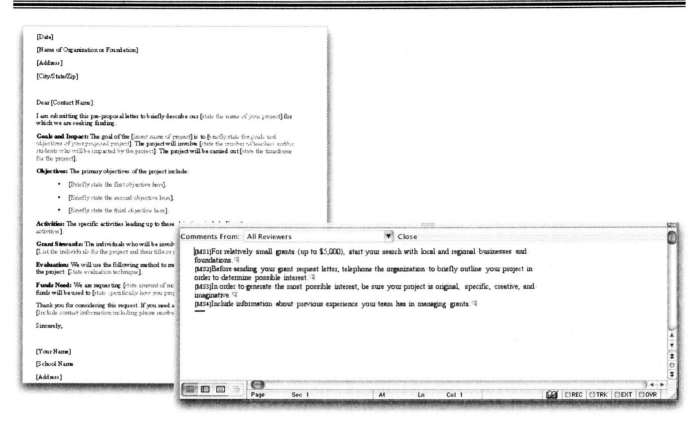

Software Application

Microsoft Word

Using the Template

1. The Grant Request Letter has comments embedded in it, which are there to provide tips that you can use while writing your letter. They appear as highlighted text in the document. Comments do not appear when a document is printed.

2. To read a comment, move your mouse over the highlighted text.

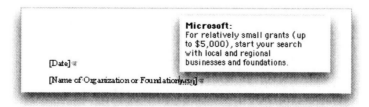

3. You can also double-click a comment to read it. This will open a split screen showing the comments in the order in which they appear. Click **Close** when you are finished reading the comments.

3. To create your own letter, select the text, including the brackets that surround it, and type your own information.

Grant Request Letter *(cont.)*

Tips and Tricks

- To change the font type, size, or style, select the text you wish to change (or use the **Edit→Select All** menu to select the entire document). Go to the **Format→Font** menu and make your changes.

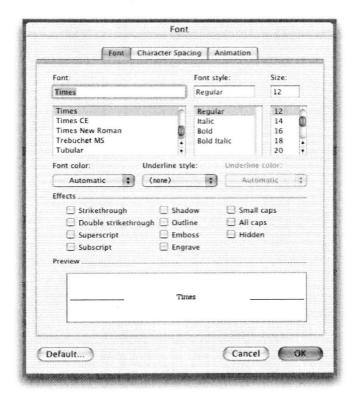

- If you would like to add a border to the page, go to **Format→Borders and Shading** and select the **Page Border** tab. Select a line style and width for your border, or click the Art pull-down menu to select an art border.

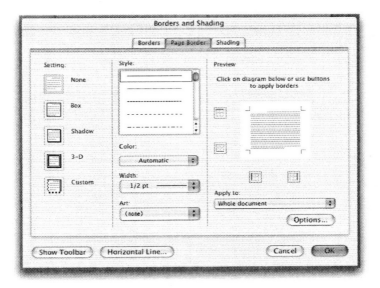

Graph Paper

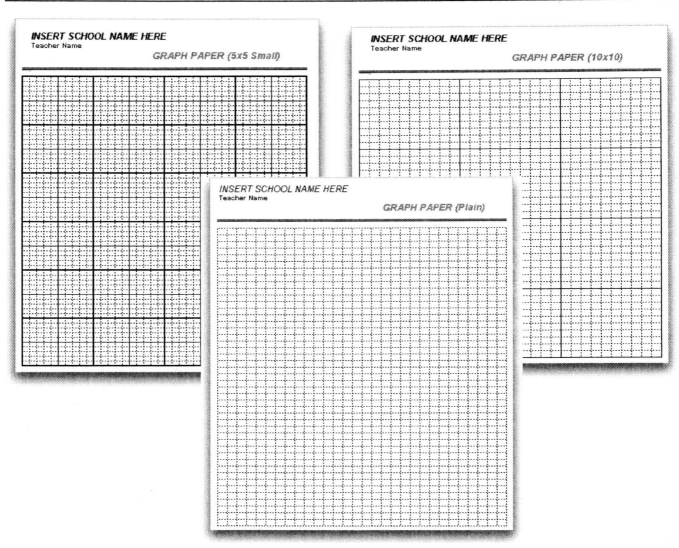

Software Application

Microsoft Excel

Using the Template

1. The Graph Paper template has five different sizes of graph paper—5 x 5, 10 x 10, Plain Large, and 5 x 5 Small. Each size appears on its own worksheet. To select a worksheet, click its tab at the bottom of the page.

2. Replace the **Insert School Name Here** and **Teacher Name** text at the top of each worksheet with your school name and teacher name.

Graph Paper *(cont.)*

Tips and Tricks

- To view column and row headers, go to **Tools→Preferences** (or **Excel→Preferences** if you are using *Excel XP* or *X*) and select the box beside **Row & Column Headers**.

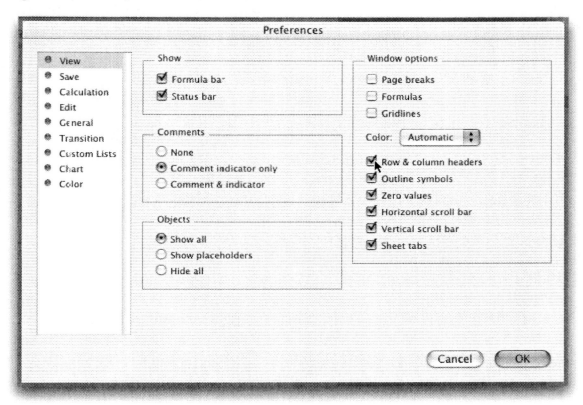

- To change the view of the template on your screen, go to the **Zoom** pull-down menu and select a different percentage. This does not affect how the template prints.

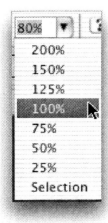

- See page 110 for extension ideas on how to use graph paper in the classroom.

Hall Pass

Insert Name of School Here

OFFICE PASS

_____ has my permission
to be in the hallways to go to and from the school office only.

Date: _____

Time: _____

_____
Teacher's Name

Insert Name of School Here

RESTROOM PASS

_____ has my permission
to be in the hallways to go to and from the restroom only.

Date: _____

Time: _____

_____
Teacher's Name

Software Application

Microsoft Word

Using the Template

1. Decide which pass to use and highlight the **Insert Name of School Here** text. Type your school name.

2. Click the first blank line. Type the student's name.

3. Click the following lines to type the date, time, and teacher's name.

Inventory Control

Insert Name of School Here							
Year/Semester				INVENTORY CONTROL			
Item	**Location**	**Make**	**Model**	**Serial No.**	**Price**	**Purchased**	**Other**

Software Application

Microsoft Excel

Using the Template

1. Select the **Insert School Name Here** text. Type the name of your school.

2. Select the **Year/Semester** text and replace it with the current year and/or semester.

3. Type the information into the worksheet. If you need to increase the size of any of the columns or rows, move your mouse to the line between two columns or rows until the pointer becomes a double-headed arrow.

4. Click the mouse and drag to increase or decrease the row or column size.

Lesson Plan

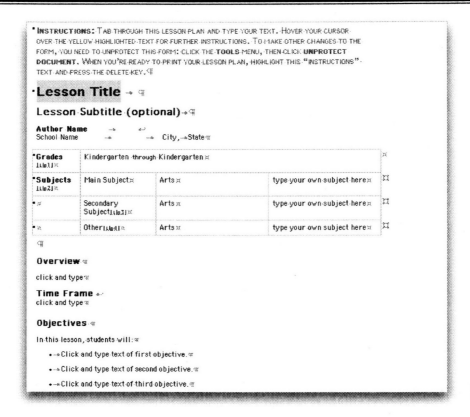

Software Application

Microsoft Word

Using the Template

1. The Lesson Plan template is a standard lesson plan form with six pages. Included is space for objectives, national standards, student activity sheet, contact information, and more. Instructions for using the template appear in blue at the top of the document. You will need to delete them before printing the lesson plan; however, they will come in handy while working with the document.

2. Text that appears highlighted in yellow has comments attached. In this instance, the comments provide additional information on using the template. To view the comments, hover your mouse over the highlighted text and wait for the comment to appear.

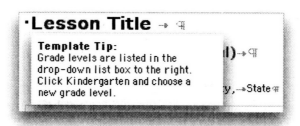

Lesson Plan *(cont.)*

3. Type the lesson title and the subtitle, if you have one. If you do not have a subtitle, you can delete that line from the document. For the lines below, type the author name, school name, and city and state.

4. In the table, select the grades and subjects. To select a grade, click the word **Kindergarten** in the table and select a grade level from the pull-down menu that appears. Select any other grade level and subject area from the remaining pull-down menus.

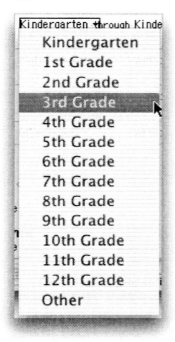

5. Type your own subject area in the last column or delete the text if you do not need it for your document.

6. To make any other changes to the template, you will need to unprotect the document. Go to the **Tools** menu and select **Unprotect Document**.

Lists and Charts

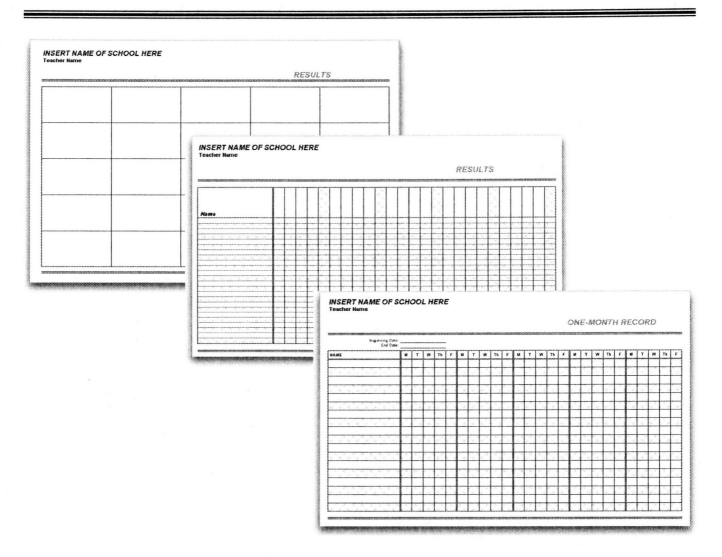

Software Application

Microsoft Excel

Using the Template

1. The Lists and Charts template consists of three worksheets—Vertical, Plain Grid, and One-Month Record. Use the tabs at the bottom of the page to select the worksheet you want to use.

2. Select the **Insert Name of School Here** and **Teacher Name** text and replace it with your school and teacher information.

3. For the One-Month Record template, type a beginning date and an ending date.

Medication Dispensing (Authorization)

Insert Name of School Here

MEDICATION AUTHORIZATION

Student's Name: _____ Date: _____

Teacher's Name: _____ Room No. _____

Part I: To be completed by Parent/Guardian

I authorize the school medical personnel to see that my child, _____,

receives the medication prescribed by _____. *(See below.)*

_____

(Parent's /Guardian's Name --Please print)   *(Phone Number)*

_____

(Parent's /Guardian's Signature)   *(Date)*

Please list all medications that your child is taking at home:

_____

Part II: To be completed by Physician

Diagnosis: _____

_____

(Medication)   *(Dosage)*   *(Route of administration)*   *(Time/Frequency)*

If PRN, state frequency or indication: _____

Duration of Treatment: _____

Possible Side Effects and Adverse Reaction: _____

Other Recommendations: _____

_____

Is this drug covered by the psychotropic drug law? ____Yes   ____No

_____

(Physician's Name -- Please print)   *(Phone Number)*   *(FAX Number)*

_____

(Physician's Signature)   *(Date)*

Software Application

Microsoft Word

Using the Template

1. Select the **Insert Name of School Here** text and replace it with the name of your school.

2. Click in each field and type the student's name, the date, the teacher's name, and the room number.

3. Print the document.

Music Paper

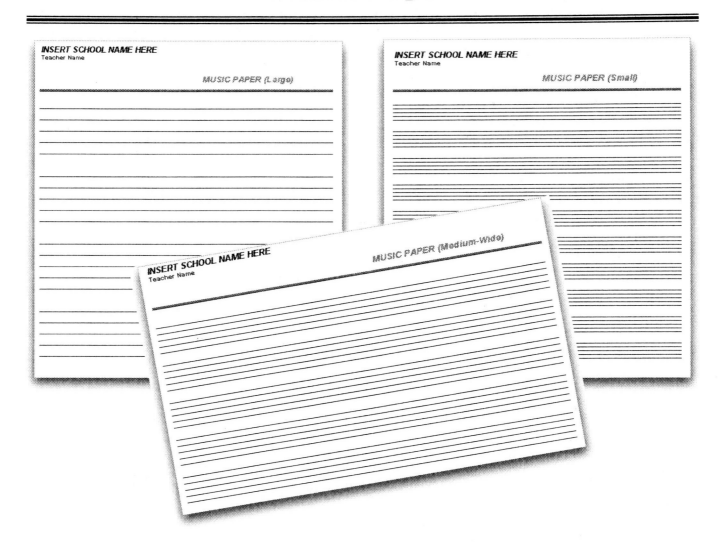

Software Application

Microsoft Excel

Using the Template

1. The Music Paper workbook has templates in three different sizes—small, medium, and large. Each is formatted to print in Portrait, or vertical, format. Each template also has a wide version, which prints in Landscape, or horizontal, format.

2. To select the worksheet you wish to use, click the tabs at the bottom of the workbook.

3. Select the **Insert School Name Here** text. Type the name of your school. Select the **Teacher Name** text and replace it with the teacher's name.

Newsletter Wizard

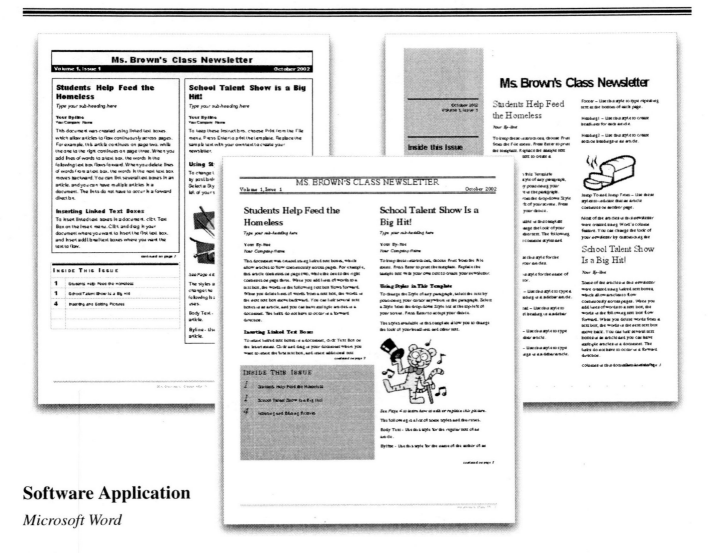

Software Application

Microsoft Word

Using the Template

1. The Newsletter Wizard takes you through a step-by-step process to create a newsletter. When you open the template, the first dialog box appears. Click the **Next** button to continue.

Newsletter Wizard *(cont.)*

2. At the next dialog box, choose the format you want for your newsletter—Professional, Contemporary, or Elegant. You can also choose whether you want your newsletter to be in black and white or color.

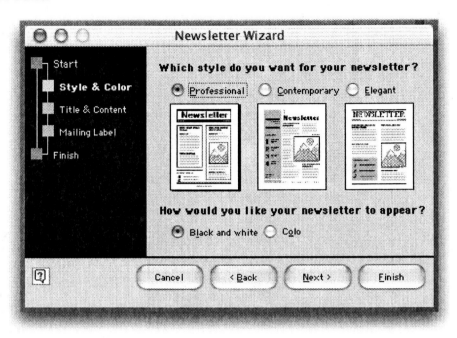

3. Next, type the title of your newsletter. You can always change it later if you are not sure what you want the title to be. If you want to include the date, check the box next to "Date." Type any changes to the date in the box beside it. If you want to include the Volume and Issue number, check the box and make any necessary changes. Click the **Next** button to continue.

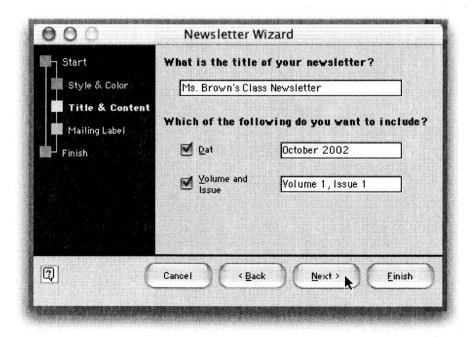

Newsletter Wizard *(cont.)*

4. At the next dialog box, you can decide if you want to leave room for a mailing label on the back of your newsletter. Click **Next** to continue.

5. Now you're finished and ready to see your newsletter! Click **Finish** to exit the Newsletter Wizard.

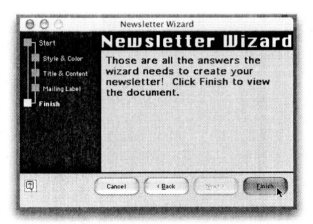

6. You might get a warning that *Word* has truncated your title. If this is the case, you may need to play with the font size and style a bit once you start working on your newsletter.

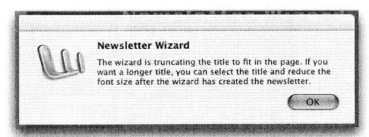

7. To personalize your newsletter, you will need to replace the text. The default text that appears in the document provides valuable tips for using the template and creating your newsletter. You might want to print out the instructions before creating the newsletter.

Overdue Book Notice

Insert Name of School Here

OVERDUE BOOK NOTICE

Name:		
Book Title:		
Author:		
Date Due:		
Price:		

Software Application

Microsoft Word

Using the Template

1. Select the **Insert Name of School Here** text and replace it with the name of your school.

2. Click in each of the sections of the notice and fill in the student's name, the name of the book, the book's author, the date the book was due, and the fine that the student will need to pay.

3. Print the page and cut out the notice to give to the student.

Tips and Tricks

- This template could also be used as an Overdue Software notice.

Insert Name of School Here

OVERDUE SOFTWARE NOTICE

Name:		
Software Title:		
Date Due:		
Fine:		

Parent Bulletin

Insert Name of School Here

PARENT BULLETIN

| Date: | |
| Class: | |

[Insert message to parent here, such as a reminder about upcoming student tests and test dates, upcoming trips, or volunteer requests, or to alert parents to a problem.]

Sincerely,

_____
(Teacher's Name)

Software Application

Microsoft Word

Using the Template

1. The Parent Bulletin template has space for the bulletin to appear twice on the page. You will have to add text and make changes in both sections of the page.

2. Select the **Insert Name of School Here** text and replace it with the name of your school.

3. Type the date and class in the table.

4. Select the text in brackets and replace with your text.

5. Type your name on the bottom line.

Parent Bulletin *(cont.)*

Modifying the Template

1. If your bulletin is not a very urgent one, or you want to use a graphic that is appropriate for a holiday or another occasion, you might want to change the graphic. To remove the existing graphic, click it to select it and press the backspace or delete key.

2. Go to the **Insert** menu and select **Picture**, then **Clip Art**.

3. When the Clip Art Gallery appears, scroll through the selections until you find a graphic that is appropriate for your bulletin. Select it and click **Insert** to add it to the document. Once you have added the graphic, you can resize it to fit in the space provided.

4. You can also change the font size and style to make the bulletin more appropriate for the occasion.

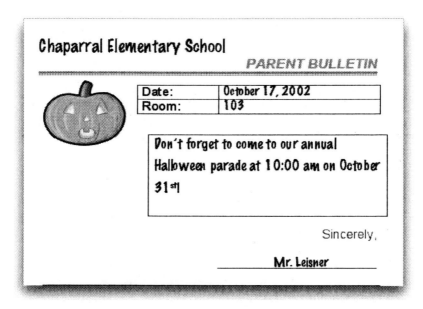

5. Don't forget to add the graphic to the lower part of the template as well. Select the art, then go to the **Edit** menu and select **Copy**. You can also use the keyboard command **Control + C** (Windows) or **Command (⌘) + C** (Macintosh). Then paste it into the lower section by going to the **Edit** menu and selecting **Paste**, or using **Control + V** (Windows) or **Command (⌘) + V** (Macintosh).

Tips and Tricks

- If you have trouble making the graphic and text appear the way that you want them, you may need to change the way that the text wraps around the graphic. Select the graphic and then click the **Format** menu. Select **Picture**. If you are using *Microsoft Word 97* or *98*, go to the **Position** tab and select **Float Over Text**. (This isn't necessary for subsequent versions of *Word*.) Then you can select how you would like the text to wrap around the picture. In this instance, you might want to select **In Front of Text** as the Wrapping Style.

Party Planner

INSERT SCHOOL NAME HERE
Teacher Name

PARTY PLANNER

Party Information

Date: _____   Number of People: _____
Time: _____   Occasion: _____
                                    Location: _____

Cost   **Budget**

Per Person: _____   Total Revenue: _____
                                        Cost per Ticket: _____
Total: _$0.00_   Total Budget: _____

Expenses

Food Total: _$0.00_   Decorations Total: _$0.0_
Food 1 _____   Decorations 1 _____
Food 2 _____   Decorations 2 _____
Food 3 _____   Decorations 3 _____
Food 4 _____   Decorations 4 _____

Beverage Total: _$0.00_   Admissions Total: _$0.0_
Beverage 1 _____   Tickets _____
Beverage 2 _____   Security _____
Beverage 3 _____   Staffing _____
Beverage 4 _____
                                        Miscellaneous Total: _$0.0_
Music Total: _$0.00_   Misc 1 _____
DJ _____   Misc 2 _____
Band _____   Misc 3 _____
                                        Misc 4 _____
Marketing Total: _$0.00_   Misc 5 _____
Invitations _____   Misc 6 _____
Posters _____   Misc 7 _____
Newspaper _____   Misc 8 _____

Claremont Junior High School
Ms. Evans

PARTY PLANNER

Party Information

Date: _12/22/02_   Number of People: _100_
Time: _6:00 PM_   Occasion: _Holiday Party_
                                    Location: _Auditorium_

Cost   **Budget**

Per Person: _$10.40_   Total Revenue: _$1,000.00_
                                        Cost per Ticket: _$10.00_
Total: _$1,040.00_   Total Budget: _$1,000.00_

Expenses

Food Total: _$300.00_   Decorations Total: _$75.00_
Food 1 _$250.00_   Decorations 1 _75.00_
Food 2 _$50.00_   Decorations 2 _____
Food 3 _____   Decorations 3 _____
Food 4 _____   Decorations 4 _____

Beverage Total: _$250.00_   Admissions Total: _$15.00_
Beverage 1 _$100.00_   Tickets _$15.00_
Beverage 2 _$150.00_   Security _____
Beverage 3 _____   Staffing _____
Beverage 4 _____
                                        Miscellaneous Total: _$50.00_
Music Total: _$300.00_   Misc 1 _$50.00_
DJ _____   Misc 2 _____
Band _$300.00_   Misc 3 _____
                                        Misc 4 _____
Marketing Total: _$50.00_   Misc 5 _____
Invitations _$50.00_   Misc 6 _____
Posters _____   Misc 7 _____
Newspaper _____   Misc 8 _____

Software Application

Microsoft Excel

Using the Template

1. Highlight the **Insert School Name Here** text and replace it with the name of your school. Highlight the **Teacher Name** text and replace it with the teacher's name.

2. The red arrows in the template indicate that comments have been attached to some of the cells. When you see a red arrow, move your mouse over the text in the cell to make the comment appear. In this case, the comments provide additional tips about adding information to the template and the calculations performed by the spreadsheet.

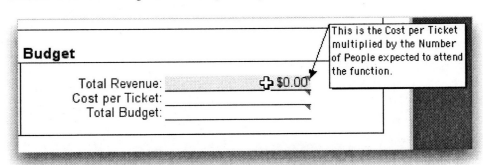

Budget

Total Revenue: ⊹ $0.00   This is the Cost per Ticket multiplied by the Number of People expected to attend the function.
Cost per Ticket: _____
Total Budget: _____

Party Planner *(cont.)*

3. Type the date, time, number of people expected, the occasion, and the location of the party. *Excel* will calculate the cost in the second section based on the expected number of people.

Party Information

Date:	12/22/02	Number of People:	100
Time:	6:00 PM	Occasion:	Holiday Party
		Location:	Auditorium

4. In the second section, three of the lines are highlighted in blue. You do not need to enter data on any of these lines. The cells indicated by these lines have formulas in them with which *Excel* will automatically calculate cost and totals. In this section, you will only need to enter data for the cost per ticket and your budget for the event.

Cost		**Budget**	
Per Person:	$0.00	Total Revenue:	$1,000.00
		Cost per Ticket:	$10.00
Total:	$0.00	Total Budget:	$1,000.00

5. In the third section, enter the cost of your expenses. Enter the cost of each expense on its own line. *Excel* will automatically calculate the total at the top of the column for each expense.

Food Total:	$300.00
Food 1	$250.00
Food 2	$50.00
Food 3	
Food 4	

6. The data that you enter for the expenses will effect the cost per person and the cost total, and can help you to determine if you need to cut costs or increase ticket prices.

Per Person:	$10.40
Total:	$1,040.00

Polls and Surveys

Software Application

Microsoft Word

Using the Template

1. The Polls and Surveys template consists of three surveys—Importance Scale, Quality Comparison, and Quality Scale. Each survey is its own separate page in the document. Scroll down until you find the survey you wish to use.

2. Make any changes to the information at the top of the page, such as replace "Gender" with "Grade," or delete a line.

3. To add your own information to the template, click in the section that reads **Add Your Own Question**, **Item Description**, or **Insert an Item Description or leave blank**. Type your own information to replace it.

4. Print the survey and make as many copies as necessary. Have each person surveyed use the scale to determine his or her answer.

Recognition Certificates

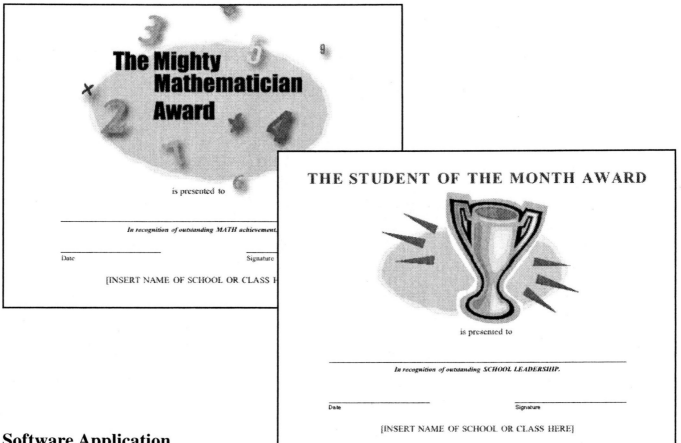

Software Application

Microsoft Word

Using the Template

1. Certificates provided in the template include the Read-a-Book-a-Week Award, Mighty Mathematician Award, Pillar of Society Award, The Sensational Scientist Award, The Stellar Speller Award, and the Student of the Month Award. Scroll down to find the template you wish to use.

2. Use the mouse to select the words "Insert Name of School or Class Here." Make sure that you have selected the brackets along with the text. Type the name of your school or class.

3. To enter a student's name, click the mouse on the first line. Type the student's name. To increase the font size or change the font style, use the mouse to select the name, then use the Formatting Toolbar or the **Format→Font** menu to make your changes.

4. Click the Date line and type the date for the award.

5. To print the file, click the printer icon in the toolbar or select **File→Print**. The template is formatted to print in landscape, or horizontal, orientation. For best results, print this template on a color printer.

Recognition Certificates *(cont.)*

Modifying the Template

- The text on the Pillar of Society Award, the Sensational Scientist Award, or the Student of the Month Award can be modified, if desired. You can also replace the text and graphic on a certificate to represent one of your classroom objectives. For example, you could modify the Sensational Scientist Award to create a Social Studies Achievement Award.

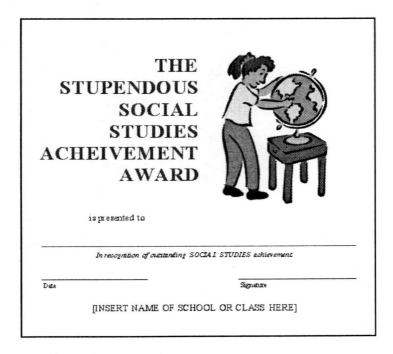

THE STUPENDOUS SOCIAL STUDIES ACHEIVEMENT AWARD

is presented to

_____

In recognition of outstanding SOCIAL STUDIES achievement

_____   _____
Date   Signature

[INSERT NAME OF SCHOOL OR CLASS HERE]

To replace a graphic, use the mouse to select the existing graphic and press backspace or delete on your keyboard. Go to the **Insert** menu and select **Picture**.

If you would like to use a graphic from the clip art gallery that comes with *Microsoft Office*, select **Clip Art**. The Clip Art Gallery will open. Look through the categories until you find a graphic that is appropriate for your award. Select the graphic and click **Insert** to add it to your document. Close the Clip Art Gallery to return to *Microsoft Word*.

If you have a graphic in your files that you would like to use, select **From File**. Locate the graphic you wish to use and click **Insert** to add it to your document.

Once you have added the graphic, select it with the mouse and drag it into the area of the award in which you want it to appear. You can then use the mouse to resize it. Click a grabber handle and drag the mouse until the graphic is the size that you want.

Tips and Tricks

- If you have trouble moving your graphic, select the graphic and then click the **Format** menu. Select **Picture**. If you are using *Microsoft Word 97* or *98*, go to the **Position** tab and select **Float Over Text**. (This step is not needed for later versions of *Word*.) Then you can select how you would like the text to wrap around the picture.

Requisition Form

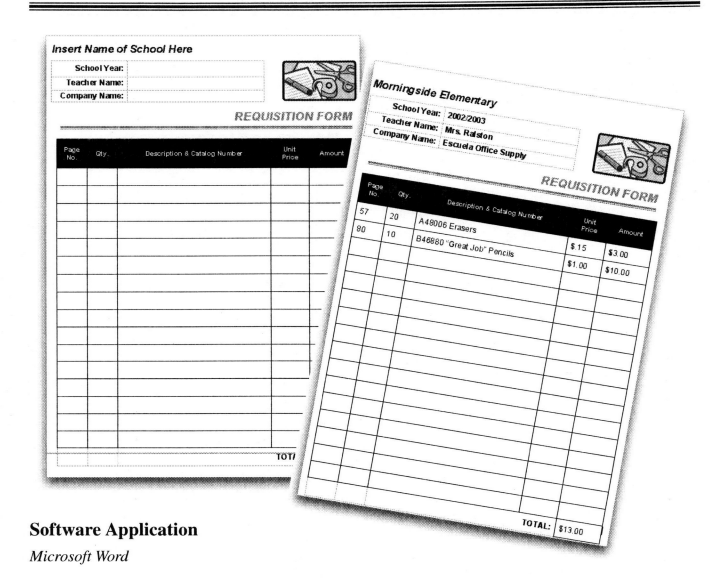

Software Application

Microsoft Word

Using the Template

1. Use the Requisition Form template to order books, office supplies, and other materials for your classroom. Highlight the **Insert Name of School Here** text and replace it with the name of your school.

2. Type the school year, teacher name, and the name of the company from which you are ordering in the lines at the beginning of the page.

3. Click inside the table to begin filling out your order. Type the page number the item is on in the catalog and press the **Tab** key to move to the next section of the table.

4. Type the quantity of the item and press **Tab** to go to the next section.

5. Type the Description and Catalog Number of the item and press **Tab**.

6. Type the Unit Price and press **Tab**.

Requisition Form *(cont.)*

7. Calculate the total amount of the item and enter it in the final column. Press **Tab** to go to the beginning of the next line.

8. Repeat Steps 3–7 for the remaining items you wish to add to the form.

9. When you have entered all the items you are requesting, add the total cost amount in the **TOTAL:** line at the bottom of the table.

Tips and Tricks

- If you want *Word* to automatically calculate the total of your order, click the cell beside the **TOTAL:** line. Go to the **Table** menu and select **Formula...**.

  Word will suggest the =SUM(ABOVE) formula, which adds the total of the cells in the column above the selected cell. Click **OK**.

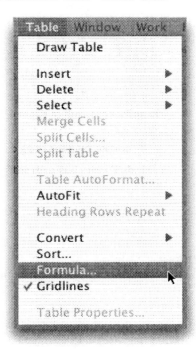 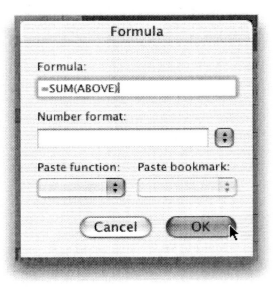

If the total does not appear correctly, you may need to type zeros in any blank cells. You may need to repeat these steps if you make any changes in the column.

Schedules

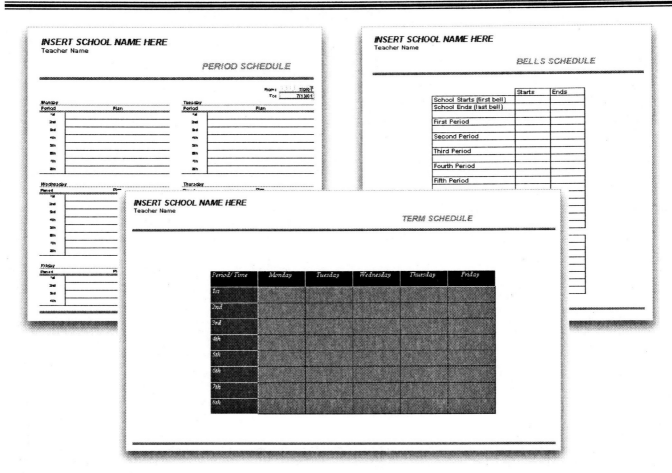

Software Application

Microsoft Excel

Using the Template

1. The Schedules template has four separate worksheets with different schedule options—By Period, By Time, Bells, and Term. To select a worksheet, click its tab at the bottom of the workbook.

2. Select the **Insert School Name Here** text and replace it with the name of your school. Select the **Teacher Name** text and replace it with the teacher's name.

3. If you are using the By Period Schedule or the By Time Schedule, type the starting date in the **From:** line. The red arrow that appears in this cell indicates that a comment is attached. To view the comment, move the mouse over the cell. In this case, the comment tells you that if you enter the date of the Monday of the week, *Excel* will automatically add the Friday.

4. Type your schedule into the spaces provided.

Schedules *(cont.)*

Tips and Tricks

- When you open the worksheet, you may get a warning about Macros in the document. Select **Enable Macros**. If you disable the macros, the worksheet will not work correctly.

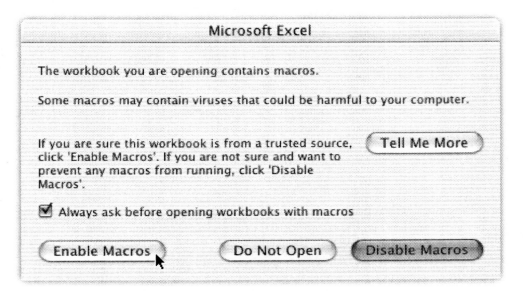

- If the workbook opens at a size that is too small for you to view, go to the zoom menu and select a new view percentage. This will not affect how the document prints.

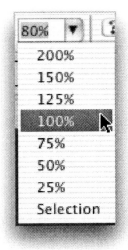

School Certificates

Software Application

Microsoft PowerPoint

Using the Template

1. There are three certificates in the School Certificates template—Professional Development, Certificate of Excellence, and The Red Ribbon Award. Each certificate appears on its own slide. Scroll down to select the template you wish to use.

2. Select the **[Insert Name of School Here]** text, including the brackets, and replace it with the name of your school.

3. Select and replace the remaining text that appears in brackets in the document.

4. You can either type the name of the award winner before printing, or write it in afterwards.

School Certificates *(cont.)*

Tips and Tricks

- If you are using the Professional Development Certificate and printing the certificate in color, you may want the **[Insert Professional Development Topic]** text to appear in red. Select the text you typed and select the color red from the Font Color options.

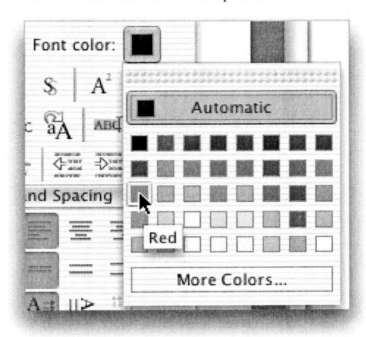

- If you are using The Red Ribbon Award, and you are typing the name of the award recipient before printing, you might notice that when you type the name, the line moves to the right.

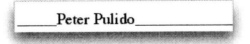

One way to keep the line under the text is to create a text box above the line rather than type on the line. To do this, first make sure that the Drawing Toolbar is visible. If it is not, go to the **View** menu and select **Toolbars→Drawing**.

Select the textbox tool and drag a textbox over the line. Type the name in the box. You may need to increase the font size of the text.

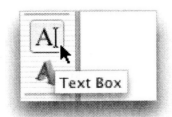

Seating Chart

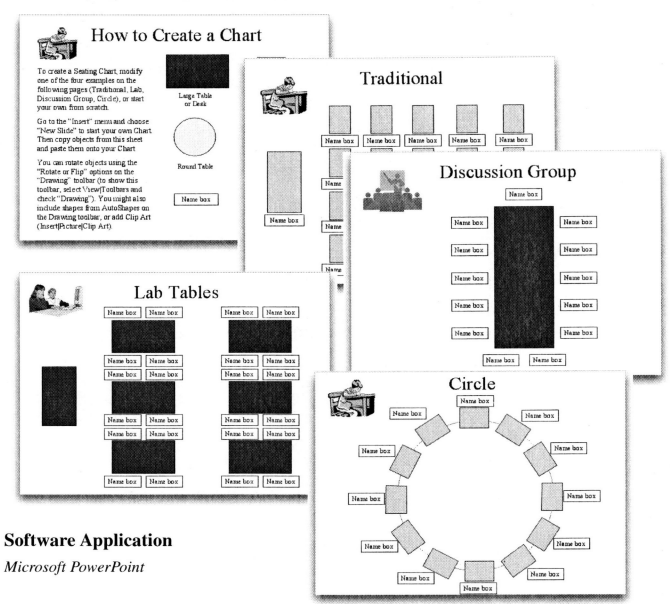

Software Application

Microsoft PowerPoint

Using the Template

1. With the Seating Chart Template, you can either follow the directions to create your own seating chart, or use one of the four options provided—Traditional, Discussion Group, Lab Tables, or Circle. Each example appears on its own slide. Scroll down to view all the options.

2. If you are using one of the provided options, you will only need to add names. Click inside one of the name boxes and select the **Name Box** text. Type the student's name. If you are adding both first and last names, you may need to make the font size smaller.

3. If you are creating your own seating chart, insert a blank slide in the document on which you can create your chart. Go to the **Insert** menu and select **New Slide**. Then you can copy and paste the symbols from the first slide onto this new slide.

Seating Chart *(cont.)*

Tips and Tricks

- If you are creating your own seating chart, it might be easiest to create a new presentation. That way, you could keep both documents open on the screen at the same time, making for easier copying and pasting. First, make sure that you are in Slide view. You can use the buttons at the bottom left-hand side of the document to change the view.

Make the seating chart presentation window small enough so that it only takes up half the space on your screen. You can make a window smaller by clicking the lower right corner of the window and dragging towards the upper left.

Go to **File** and select **New Presentation**. Select a **Blank Presentation**.

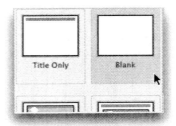

Once you have the new document open, make that window smaller, too, and place it beside the Seating Chart template. Use your mouse to drag objects from the template to your new document. Then you can arrange them according to your preferred seating plan.

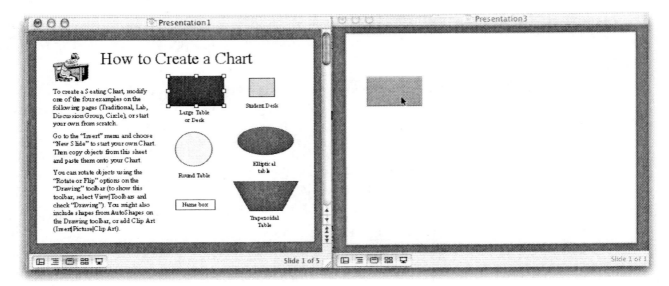

Student Behavior Contract

Insert Name of School Here

STUDENT BEHAVIOR CONTRACT

DATE _____

Dear _____

Today I had a problem in school:

What I did: _____

_____

_____

What happened because I did what I did: _____

_____

_____

What I should have done: _____

_____

_____

What would have happened if I had done what I should have done: _____

_____

_____

I need to talk to you about my plan for how to handle a similar problem next time. Please sign this. I need to bring it back to school immediately.

_____
Student Signature

_____
Teacher Signature

_____
Parent Signature

Parent Comments: _____

_____

_____

Software Application

Microsoft Word

Using the Template

1. Select the **Insert Name of School Here** text and replace it with the name of your school.

2. Print the template and distribute it to students when necessary.

Student Database

INSERT NAME OF SCHOOL HERE

STUDENT DATABASE

Student Name	Contact	Phone	Birthday	Medication/Special Needs	Other

Software Application

Microsoft Excel

Using the Template

1. Select the **Insert School Name Here** text. Type the name of your school.
2. Type the names of your students and their information into the rows provided.
3. If you want to sort the information that you have entered, go to the **Data** menu and select **Sort**.

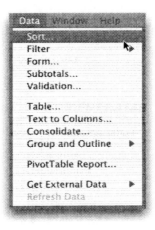

Student Database *(cont.)*

4. *Excel* automatically selects the name of the first column, **Student Name**. (If you don't see the name of the column, make sure that in the **My List Has** section, the box or circle beside **Header row** is selected.)

5. If you want to sort by a different criteria, click **Student Name** and select a different column name.

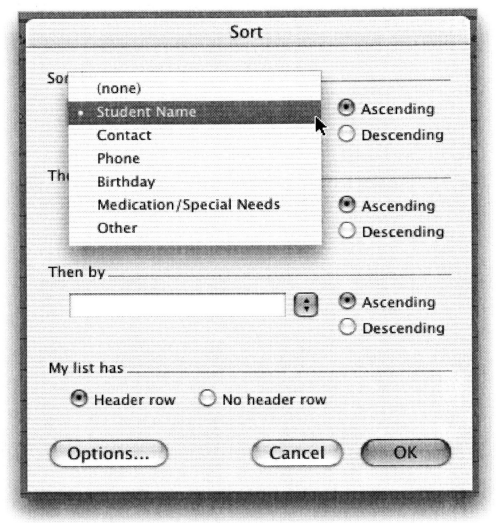

6. If you want to sort from A–Z, select the circle or box next to **Ascending**. If you want to sort from Z–A, select the circle or box next to **Descending**.

7. Click **OK** to sort your data.

Student Disciplinary Action

Insert Name of School Here

STUDENT DISCIPLINARY ACTION

STUDENT NAME:		ID#	

GRADE:	

INFRACTION:

Date:	
Time:	
Location	

DESCRIPTION:

DISCIPLINARY ACTION TAKEN:

TEACHER:		DATE:	
STUDENT:		DATE:	
PARENT:		DATE:	
DISCIPLINARY AGENT:		DATE:	

Software Application

Microsoft Word

Modifying the Template

1. Select the **Insert School Name Here** text. Type the name of your school.

2. Type the student's name, ID#, and grade in the spaces provided.

3. Type the date, time, and location of the infraction.

4. Type a description of the event. The box will expand to fit the text that you type.

5. Type the disciplinary action taken. This box will also expand to fit your text.

6. Print the page and sign it.

Student Note

Insert Name of School Here

STUDENT NOTE

STUDENT'S NAME: _____   DATE _____

TEACHER'S NAME: _____

_____ **Absent/Late**   My child was _____ absent or _____ late on _____.

Reason: _____

_____

_____ **Dismissal**   Please dismiss my child from school at _____ on

_____ for the following reason: _____

_____

_____ **Permission**   After school my child has permission to: [state specific activity]:

_____

_____

_____

_____ **Comments**   _____

_____

_____

_____

Parent/Guardian
Name (Please Print) _____

Signature   X_____

Software Application

Microsoft Word

Using the Template

1. Select the **Insert School Name Here** text. Type the name of your school.

2. Print the student note and provide it for parents to use when necessary.

Substitute Teacher Form

INSERT NAME OF SCHOOL HERE
Teacher Name
Class

SUBSTITUTE TEACHER INFORMATION

Administration Information:

Principal: _____   Other Support: _____
Paraprofessional: _____   _____
Team Teacher: _____   _____

Notes and Suggestions

Notes: _____
_____
_____

Suggestions: _____
_____

Time Fillers: _____
_____
_____
_____
_____

Daily Schedule

Time Begin - End	

Software Application

Microsoft Excel

Using the Template

1. Select the **Insert School Name Here** text. Type the name of your school.

2. Select the **Teacher Name** and **Class** text and replace it with your information.

3. Type the information for the substitute teacher and print the page.

Tips and Tricks

- When you open the worksheet, you may get a warning about Macros in the document. Select **Enable Macros**. If you disable the macros, the document will not work correctly.

Syllabus

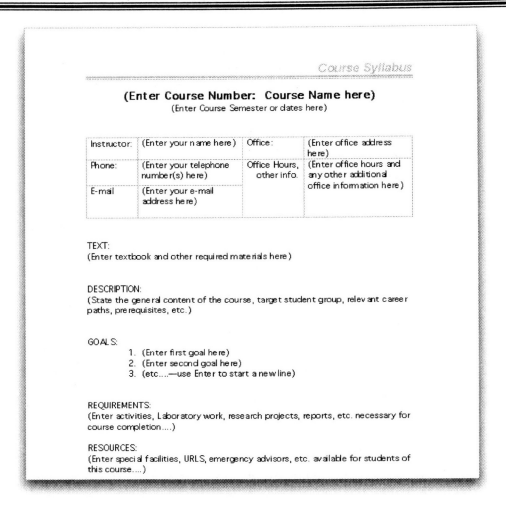

Software Application

Microsoft Word

Using the Template

1. When you open the Syllabus template, a series of dialog boxes appear. Enter the information requested and click **OK**.

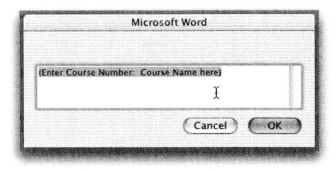

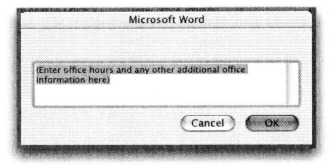

Syllabus *(cont.)*

2. If any of the information requested does not apply, just click **OK** in the dialog box. You can delete that section on the syllabus once *Word* has personalized it for you.

3. Once you have entered your information, *Word* formats the syllabus for you complete with your information. You can edit any of the text after it has been entered into the document.

4. The second page of the syllabus has a chart which you can complete with your course schedule. The first line of the chart header is highlighted in yellow, indicating that a comment has been attached. Hold your mouse over the highlighted text to view the comment. (MOCT refers to "Microsoft Office Comment.")

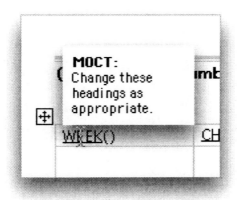

Tests

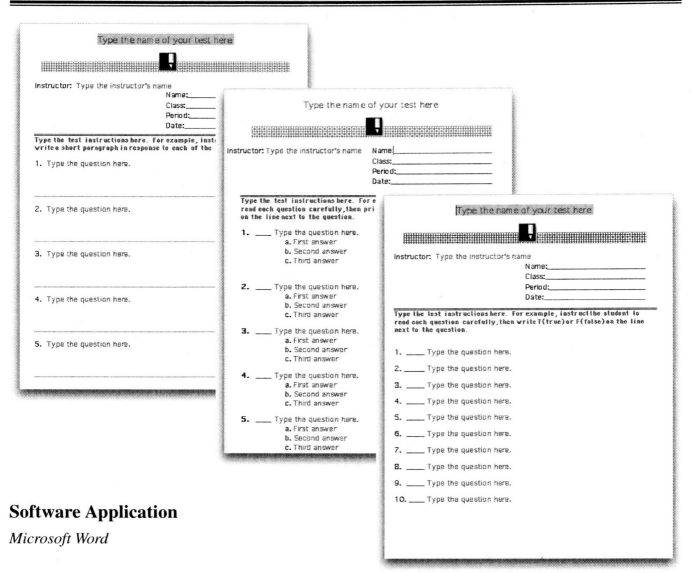

Software Application

Microsoft Word

Modifying the Template

1. When you open the Tests template, a dialog box appears. Select the type of test you want to create—essay, multiple choice, or true/false—and click **OK**.

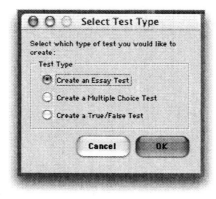

Tests *(cont.)*

2. A test appears in the format you requested. Type the name of the test in the line at the top of the page.

3. The text that appears in blue has instructions for creating the text. Select it and replace it with your own text.

4. Print your test.

United States History Test

Instructor: Mr. Olmedo

Name:_____
Class:_____
Period:_____
Date:_____

Directions: Read the questions, and choose the best answer. Print the letter of the correct answer on the line beside the question.

1. ____ Why did the first group of settlers come to the New World?
   a. to look for gold
   b. to practice their religion openly
   c. to find a new route to the East Indies

2. ____ The original thirteen states had been _____ of Great Britain.
   a. territories
   b. kingdoms
   c. colonies

3. ____ Where was the declaration of Independence signed?
   a. New York City
   b. Washington, D.C.
   c. Philadelphia, Pennsylvania

4. ____ The purpose of building canals was to
   a. speed the movement of people and products
   b. spread fishing throughout the states
   c. irrigate farmlands

5. ____ Which of the following is an example of an import?
   a. glass sent from Pittsburg to Detroit
   b. a car made in Germany and shipped to New York
   c. corn sent from Illinois to Russia

Thesis

[TYPE THESIS TITLE HERE]

by

[Your Name]

A thesis submitted in partial fulfillment
of the requirements for the degree of

[Name of degree]

[Name of university]

[Year]

Approved by _____
Chairperson of Supervisory Committee

_____
_____
_____

Program Authorized
to Offer Degree _____

Date _____

Software Application

Microsoft Word

Using the Template

1. The Thesis template is a four-page guide for organizing a thesis. It has sections for a title page, abstract, table of contents, list of figures, acknowledgements, glossary, chapters, bibliography, and index.

Thesis *(cont.)*

2. If you need to add additional pages, go to **Insert** and select **Break**, then **Page Break**, or use the keyboard commands—**Control + Enter** for Windows, or **Shift + Enter** for Macintosh.

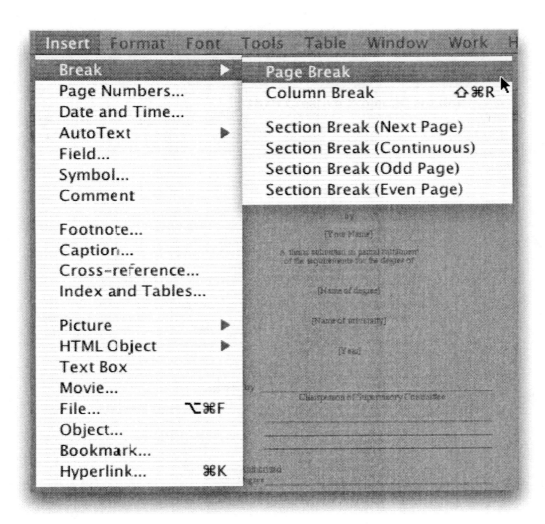

To Do List

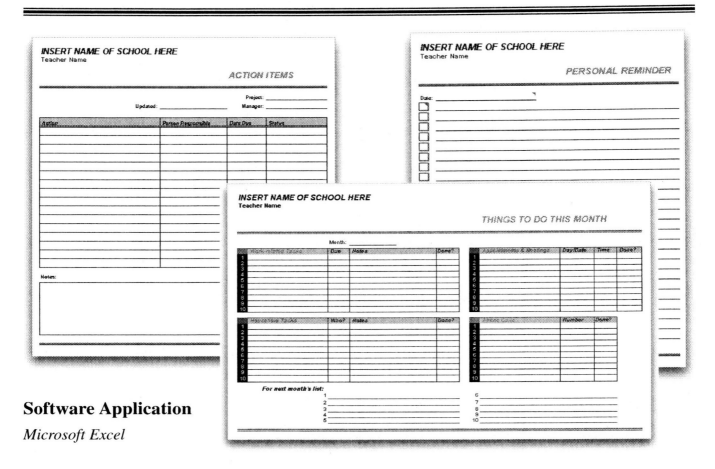

Software Application

Microsoft Excel

Using the Template

1. The To Do List template has three options—Personal Reminder, Action Items, and Things to Do This Month. Click the tab to select a worksheet.

2. Select the **Insert School Name Here** text. Type the name of your school.

3. The **Personal Reminder** worksheet has comments attached. The red arrows in the cells indicate that there is a comment. To view the comment, hold your mouse over the cell.

4. You can either type the information in *Excel* or print and write by hand.

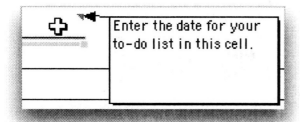

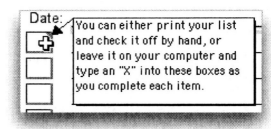

Wise Reward

Insert Name of School Here

A WISE REWARD

Hey, _____. I was
watching you. I saw you helping another student.
That shows caring for other____ ____ _____ __ _____
of yourself for being so wis__

Insert Name of School Here

A WISE REWARD

Hey, _____ I was
watching you. After lunch I saw you helping to
clean up. That shows good citizenship. You should
be proud of yourself for being so wise.

Insert Name of School Here

A WISE REWARD

Hey, _____ I was
watching you. During recess you let someone else
have a turn on the playground equipment. That
shows fairness. You should t_____
for being so wise.

Insert Name of School Here

A WISE REWARD

Hey, _____ I was
watching you. During the school assembly, you
listened carefully. That shows respect for others.
You should be proud of yourself for being so wise.

Software Application

Microsoft Word

Using the Template

1. The Wise Rewards template has rewards for caring, citizenship, fairness, and respect. Scroll through the page to view the templates.

2. Click the line to type the student's name. The line stretches to accommodate your text. Use the backspace or delete key to delete the excess line. You could also print the page and write the student's name by hand.

3. Print the reward, cut it out, and give it to the student.

Modifying the Template

- You could change the picture or the text of any of the rewards to suit your needs. If you want to add a picture, start by deleting the existing picture. Click it to select it and press the delete or backspace key.

Wise Reward *(cont.)*

Go to the **Insert** menu and select **Picture**, then **Clip Art**. The Microsoft Clip Gallery will appear. You can either scroll through the categories or type a word into the **Search** box.

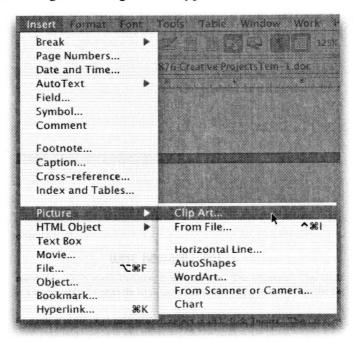

When you find the graphic you want to add, select it and click **Insert**. Then you can adjust the size to fit it in the space provided.

If you have trouble moving the picture, you may need to format it differently. Click the picture to select it. Go to the **Format** menu and select **Picture**. If you are using *Word 97* or *98*, go to the **Position** tab and select **Float Over Text**. (This isn't necessary if you are using *Word 2000/2001* or *XP/X*.) Then you can select how you would like the text to wrap around the picture. (In this case, you might want to select **In Front of Text** as the wrapping option.)

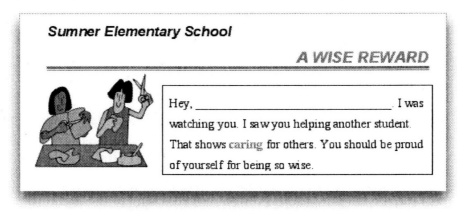

Tips and Tricks

- When you open the worksheet, you may get a warning about Macros in the document. Select **Enable Macros**. If you disable the macros, the document will not work correctly.

Writing Rubric

Insert Name of School Here

NOTE: The specific criteria for each category are meant to serve only as a guide. You may want to insert your own criteria based on your own standards. *Delete this text box before printing.*

WRITING RUBRIC

CATEGORY	4	3	2	1
Topic Sentence	Each paragraph starts with a well-constructed and focused topic sentence.	Almost all paragraphs start with a well-constructed topic sentence.	The topic sentences are not well constructed and they don't focus on one topic.	Paragraphs do not start with a sentence with a focused topic.
Supporting Details	Each paragraph contains 2 or 3 details that support the topic.	Each paragraph contains at least 2 details that support the topic.	Each paragraph contains at least 1 detail that supports the topic.	Paragraphs do not contain details that support the topic.
Vocabulary	Vivid words and phrases are used that bring the topic alive and are used accurately.	Vivid words and phrases are used that bring the topic alive and they may not always be used accurately.	The vocabulary words used clearly communicate ideas but there is a lack of variety.	The vocabulary used is limited and does not adequately communicate ideas.
Grammar & Spelling	There are no errors in grammar or spelling.	There are 1 or 2 errors in grammar or spelling but they don't affect meaning.	There are 3 or 4 errors in grammar or spelling that distract the reader from the content.	There are more than 4 errors in grammar or spelling that make the paper difficult to understand.
Capitalization & Punctuation	There are no errors in capitalization or punctuation.	There are 1 or 2 errors in capitalization and/or punctuation but the paper is still easy to understand.	There are a few errors in capitalization and/or punctuation that distracts from the content.	There are more than four errors in capitalization and/or punctuation that make the paper difficult to understand.
Conclusion	The conclusion is well constructed and draws together all the details to form an ending.	There is a conclusion and it draws together most of the details.	There is a conclusion but it doesn't draw together most of the details.	There is no clear conclusion or ending to the paper.

Software Application

Microsoft Word

Using the Template

1. Select the **Insert Name of School Here** text and replace it with the name of your school.

2. Read the directions that appear in the text box underneath the school name. You can delete the directions when you no longer need them by clicking on the text box, then pressing the backspace or delete key.

3. The Writing Rubric template provides an easy method of grading students' writing assignments. If you have any additional criteria that you want to add to any of the sections, simply click in the section of the table where you want to add the information, and then type. The sections of the table will automatically expand to fit your text.

Writing Rubric *(cont.)*

Modifying the Template

- You can use this template as a guide for creating rubrics for any subject matter. For example, you could use it to grade a student's multimedia presentation or science project.

  To delete the existing text, highlight it, then go to the **Edit** menu, select **Clear**, and then **Contents**. This will delete only the text, leaving the formatting intact.

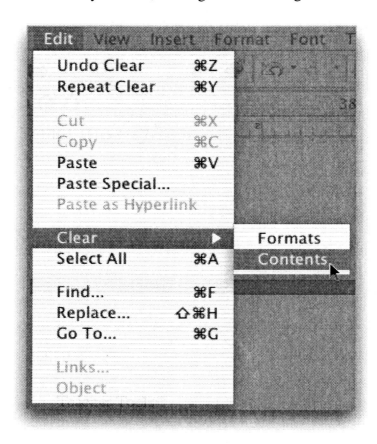

You can then type your new information into the table.

3 x 5 Research Notes

RESEARCH NOTES

Title of Report:	Water Conservation

Student Name:	Kim Van Gorp

Note Card:

Author:	Bellamy, David		Year:	
Title:	The River			
Publication:				
Publisher:	Crown		Year:	1988
Pages:	128	Library Reference:		

Summary: The chronicle of an environmental accident on a river community and its impact on animal and plant life.

Software Application

Microsoft Word

Using the Template

1. Have your students use the 3 x 5 Research Notes template to record their research project resources. Students can personalize the heading section—the **Title of the Report** and **Student Name** information—and then use the note cards to record each resource.

2. To personalize the title of the project, students can click inside the text box to the right of the **Title of Report** text box and type the name of their reports. Have them do the same for the student name portion of the heading. Students can click inside the text box to the right of the **Student Name** text box type their names. Once the heading is finished, students can proceed to the note card section.

3. Students can add pertinent information to each of the note card sections by clicking in the section box and typing in the needed information. See the example above.

3 x 5 Research Notes *(cont.)*

4. Information that has been included in the template that is not necessary can be removed. For example, you may not want your students to include the directions for filling out the note cards in the final printout. For example:

   "1. Name the source. Include all the information you'll need to identify the source..."

   To remove these lines, students can highlight the information and press the Delete or Backspace key. If they want the information back or want to change what they have deleted, have them click **Edit** on the Menu Bar and go to **Undo**.

5. Your students may want to add more note cards as they collect information. The individual note card layout was created within a table. To copy it, you will need to highlight the entire table, being careful not to include areas outside the boundaries of the table.

   If students click in the table, they will see a little box with four arrows just outside the top left-hand corner of the table. If they click this little box, the entire table will be highlighted. (Another method of selecting a table is to click on a cell in the table, go to the **Table** menu, and choose **Select Table**.) Students can **Copy** the table and **Paste** it for as many copies of the card as needed.

Tips and Tricks

- This note card style can be changed in a number of ways. For example, the card can be modified to record Internet references.

Internet Web Site Reference Card:

Name of the Site:	
Name of the Author:	
Web Address:	
Date Accessed:	
Summary of Information Used:	

- **To Delete an Entire Row:** Highlight the entire row, click on **Table**, and go down to **Delete** and across to **Rows** and click to delete.
- **To Add an Entire Row:** Decide where you want to add your row and click in a cell either above or below where you want the row to be. Go to the **Table** menu, select **Insert**, and then either **Row Above** or **Row Below**.

3 x 5 Research Notes *(cont.)*

- **To Merge Cells or Put Together Cells in the Table:** Highlight the cells to be merged. Go to the **Table** menu, and select **Merge Cells.**

- **To Split Cells into Two or More Cells:** Highlight the cell to be split, click on **Table** and go to **Split Cells.** Click and select the number or rows or columns you wish to replace the single cell.

- **Change the Size of a Row:** The size of the row can be made smaller by pulling up on its bottom line. If more space is required while entering information, the table cell will automatically add a row as needed to allow for more text. Encourage students to adjust the size of the cells when possible to conserve space and paper.

INTERNET REFERENCE CARD #: This row was added and its cells merged together.	
Name of the Site:	This cell has resulted from the merge of the three cells from the original template.
Name of the Author:	The names in the cells in the original template have been changed to suit the project.
Web Address:	
Date Accessed:	One row was deleted from the original template.
Summary of Information Used: This section was made smaller because the larger space was not needed.	

- If your students cannot record their information using the card template on the computer, then this card template or a modified card template can be printed for student use. As shown on the second page of the template example, more than one card can be copied and pasted onto a single page. Be sure to put the Project Information, Student Information and any other information like Class and/or Date at the top of your project sheet. Then copy and paste as many cards as you can fit on your page. You might find some minor size changes will allow you to put more or less on a page.

3 x 5 Research Notes *(cont.)*

Extension Ideas

- This card /template format can be used whenever multiple cards using the same format are needed for any project:

For example:

Wild Animal Cards   Famous Civil War Battle Cards

Elements of the Atomic Chart Cards   Sport Figure Statistics Cards

Famous Author Cards   Story Summary Cards

Homework or Activity Cards   Web Site Review Cards

Wild Animal Card:

Animal Name:	
Type of Animal:	
Habitat:	
Size:	
Food:	
Interesting Facts:	**Animal Pictures:**

Animal Quiz

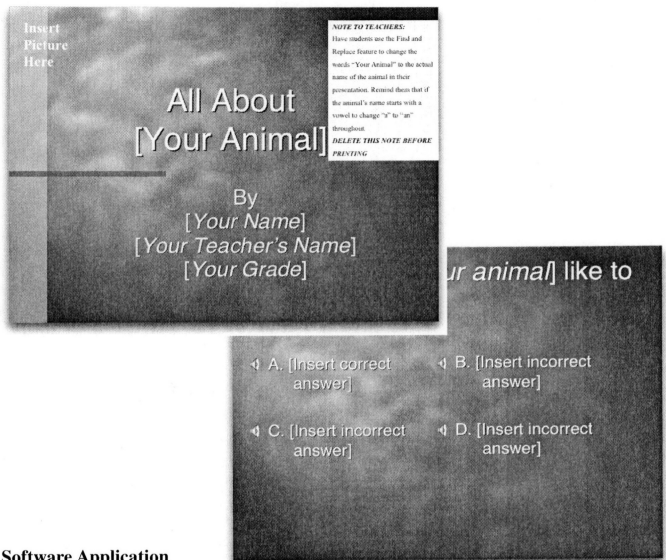

Software Application

Microsoft PowerPoint

Using the Template

1. The Animal Quiz template allows students to easily create multimedia reports. There are 17 slides in all, including information about life stages, eating habits, classification, habitat, interesting facts, and more. To view all the slides, scroll down while in Normal or Slide View.

2. The yellow text box that appears on the Animal Quiz cover has basic instructions about using the Find and Replace feature to change the words "Your Animal" to the name of the student's animal throughout the document. Follow the instructions in the text box, making sure that you include the brackets surrounding the text as well as the text itself.

3. Delete the text box by clicking on it and then pressing the backspace or delete key.

Animal Quiz *(cont.)*

4. Scroll down to the second slide. The first thing that students will need to do is make sure that the title makes sense. For example, if they replaced "[Your Animal]" with "Dolphin," the title of the second slide appears as "All About Dolphin." Have students add an "s" when necessary.

5. Double-click in the **Double click to add clip art** section of the slide. The Microsoft Clip Gallery will open. Students can scroll through the **Animals** category or type the name of their animal into the **Search:** box and click the **Search** button.

Once students see a graphic they would like to add, they can select it and click the **Insert** button to add it to the slide. Then they can use the grabber handles to adjust its size on the slide.

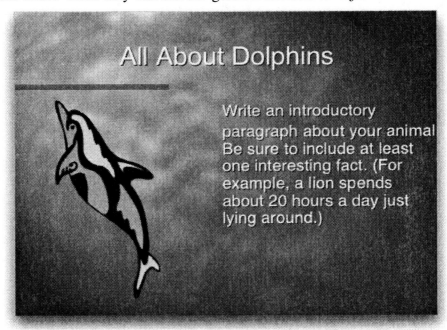

6. Have students select the paragraph that appears on the slide and press the backspace or delete key to remove the text. Make sure that they have selected the text inside the text box and not the text box itself. Then they can type their own paragraph in the space provided.

7. Once they have completed the second slide, students can scroll down to the third slide. Have them use the interesting fact that they included in the paragraph to create a quiz. For example, an interesting fact about dolphins might be that they can hold their breath for as long as 15 minutes. Students could select the **[Insert incorrect answer]** text and type something like "They can hold their breath for as long as 30 minutes." They could do the same with the remaining **[Insert incorrect answer]** options, using an incorrect number each time. Then they could replace the **[Insert correct answer]** text with the correct answer.

Animal Quiz *(cont.)*

8. If another student views the presentation, he or she can try to select the correct dolphin fact. The interactive quiz will only work in **Slide Show View**. Have the student click the sound icon to the left of the answer that he or she thinks is correct. If he or she guesses correctly, he or she will hear the sound of applause. An incorrect answer will result in the sound of a bell.

9. Have students repeat steps 4 through 8 for the remaining slides in the presentation. Each section—Classification, Habitat, Food Preferences, Life Stages, Survival, Population, and Concluding Fact—has a section for information and a quiz.

Tips and Tricks

- If you want to delete any of the slides from the presentation, select the slide either in Outline view or in Slide Sorter view. Press the backspace or delete key. If you get a message that this action will delete a slide and its contents, click **OK**.

- If students want to add a graphic from their files rather than clip art from the Microsoft Clip Gallery, have them click only once in the **Double click to add clip art** section of the slide. Then they can go to the **Insert** menu, select **Picture**, and then choose **From File**. They can navigate to their picture and press the **Insert** key to add it to the slide.

Extension Idea

- Adapt the Animal Quiz template to create presentations on plants or minerals.

Brochure

Software Application

Microsoft Word

Using the Template

1. A brochure is a document that is created in sections. This brochure template is for a tri-fold brochure. Simply stated, this template helps you to organize and place information on both sides of an 8½ x 11 sheet of paper. It divides each side of the paper into three equal sections so that when folded, each of the six sections created is the same size with the same margins and space for text and photos. Professional looking results can be obtained using card stock and printing in photo quality.

2. Provided on the template are great instructions for its use. Print the brochure's two pages and have students use them as reference while you are working on the brochure.

3. The template has two pages—a Front Brochure Page and a Back Brochure Page. Have students place their pages back to back to give them an idea of how they would look printed on both sides of one sheet. Have them fold the sections so that they can identify which section is which. The chart below shows how you would see each panel when opening the brochure.

Brochure Inside 1st Seen Panel	Brochure Back Panel	Brochure Front Panel

Brochure Inside Left Panel	Brochure Inside Center Panel	Brochure Inside Right Panel

Brochure *(cont.)*

4. Students can add text, graphics and or photos to each panel. Give students some tips on creating eye-catching, informative brochures by color coordinating text using a variety of fonts, matching borders on photos and graphics, and spacing items for effect. Creating a brochure is a creative way to have students summarize the content of a particular topic, and organize the information in a way that highlights the most important information. Higher-level thinking tasks need to be utilized here to accomplish this task.

5. To insert text, students can click inside the panel in the location where the text is to be placed. They can type the text needed, modifying its format (font, size, color, alignment, etc.) until the desired look is obtained.

6. To insert a graphic or a photo, students can click inside the panel in the location where the text is to be placed. Have them go to **Insert** on the Menu Bar and select **Picture**. If the photo or graphic has been saved on a floppy, a zip cartridge or on the hard drive, select **From File**. Locate the file, and then select **Insert**. To add clip art from the Microsoft Clip Gallery, students should select **Picture➜Clip Art**. Have them select the clip art that they would like to add and click **Insert**.

7. To add a border to a photo or graphic, students can click on the photo or graphic so that the handles are showing around the edge of the image. Have them go to the **Format** menu and select **Borders and Shading**. They can look through the options available—Setting, Style, Color Width—and select the border desired. Remind them to color coordinate photo colors with border and font colors.

8. While information about linking text boxes is given, it is generally easier to have student's think about and construct each panel or section as an individual item.

9. Once students understand the aspects of making a brochure, they can decide on the content of each panel. Have them brainstorm what the content of the brochure should be and then organize the topics so that they fit into six sections. Then they can decide on the location of each section.

   Front Section of the Brochure: Includes the title or focus of the brochure and photos or graphics that will draw attention to the brochures content.

   Back Section of the Brochure: Includes contact information so that additional information can be obtained. This information might include a map, an address, a phone number or a web or email address. This section should also include information about the creator of the brochure: student's name, class and date perhaps.

   First Inside Panel: This will be the first inside section viewed as the brochure is opened. This section is the place for important factual information and graphics or photos.

Brochure *(cont.)*

Inside Three Panels: These three panels will all be viewed at the same time so the content of each section should be related. Put the most important content section material in the middle panel and then other material in each of the side panels. Have students vary the order of the text and the photos in each panel so there is some variety in the layout of the material. Have the students make sure their eyes follow the information in a logical sequence. If eyes wander, or minds get lost, change the position of the text and photos.

An example of the content for a **U.S. State Brochure** follows. Each section gives a summary of the panel's content. Giving a copy of this to students can help them to focus their research and organize their placement of information. The teacher can determine this content outline ahead of time or students can determine the content, have it approved, and then research and create their brochure.

Panel Layout

Famous Historical Sites or Attractions 2 Photos Description of the Attractions	State Map Tourism Office Address Photo State Wildlife Student Name and Class State Nickname	State Name Graphic of State Flag State Nickname and Motto Photo of State Scene

National Park in State 2 Photos List of Activities Available in the Park.	State Sporting Activities 3 Photos of Each Caption for Each Photo	State Industries and Educational Institutions Photos of Each Statement about Each

Extension Ideas

- **Famous Author Brochure**: Have students create brochures highlighting and chronicaling an author's life, works, and contact information. The brochures could be displayed at an Author's Fair in a booth with other author-related materials.

  Other Famous brochures might include:

Inventors	Scientists
Political Leaders	Events in History
Humanitarians	Sport's Figures
Musicians	Artists

Brochure *(cont.)*

- **Holidays Around the World Brochures**: Bright and colorful would be the order of the day for these brochures. Each could feature a different holiday celebration. The brochure might include such items as a description of the holiday, foods connected with the occasion, costumes worn, folk tales related to the celebration, craft ideas, a reading list and related Web site addresses. The brochures could be displayed on a bulletin board with yarn running from the brochure to the location in the world where the holiday is frequently celebrated. This would give students a better visual connection to location of the holiday celebration.

- **How-to Brochures**: These can be fun to create, but the value lies in their helpfulness. Have students create brochures that relate to different activities they are expected to accomplish. The brochure can act as a reminder for or a guide to the activity.

Topics might include:

Using the Digital Camera	Taking Care of Your New Pet
Writing a Book Report	Analyzing a Book
Creating a Successful Science Fair Project	Making the Best Rocket
Solving Basic Algerbra Problems and Equations	Solving Math Word Problems

Calendar

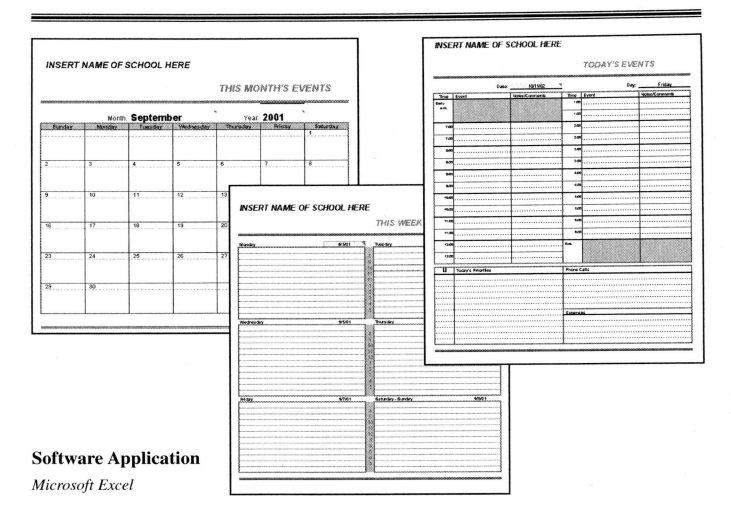

Software Application

Microsoft Excel

Using the Template

1. The Calendar template includes a calendar for monthly events, weekly events, and today's events. To select a type of calendar, students can click the tabs at the bottom of the worksheet.

2. The red arrows in the template indicate that comments are attached. The comments provide additional tips for creating the calendar. Show students how to view a comment, by holding the mouse over the cell until the comment appears.

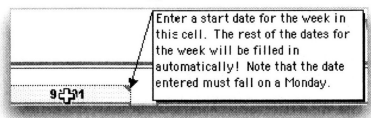

Calendar *(cont.)*

3. When students add start dates to the calendar, *Excel* will automatically fill in the day of the week for the daily calendar or the remaining dates for the week for the Weekly calendar. When students add the month and year for the monthly calendar, *Excel* will automatically fill in the days of the month accordingly. If students make any changes to the date, *Excel* will adjust the template accordingly.

Tips and Tricks

- When you open the worksheet, you may get a warning about Macros in the document. Select **Enable Macros**. If you disable the macros, the worksheet will not work correctly.
- If you have more than one event that you want to list within a cell on the monthly calendar, you can separate the text without moving to a new cell.

  If you are using a Windows computer, hold down the **Alt** key as you press **Enter**. If you are using a Macintosh computer, hold down the **command (⌘)** key and the **option** key as you press **return**.

Extension Ideas

- Create a calendar for a given month. Assign each student a date to research. Have them use the Internet to conduct their research. They can type the date and "day in history" (in quotes) in a search engine to find an event that happened that day or a celebration that occurs that day. Students can open the calendar file and type their event in the space allotted for that day.

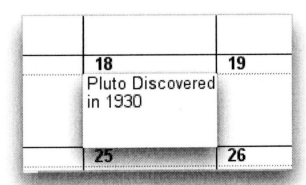

- Have students use calendars to represent time lines for a Social Studies project. Students can create a calendar for the month and year in history and type the names and dates of the events in the spaces provided.

Calendar Wizard

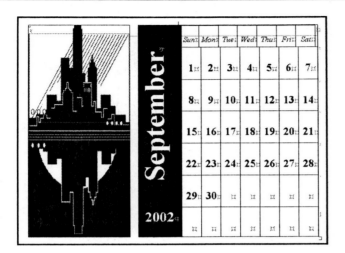

Software Application

Microsoft Word

Using the Template

1. The Calendar Wizard takes students through a step-by-step process to personalize their calendars. When they see the Start screen, have them press **Next** to continue.

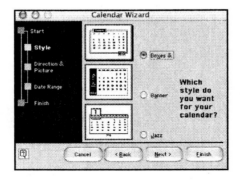

2. Students can decide what kind of style they want for their calendars. If they are going to be adding information into the calendar, they might want to select the **Boxes** style. If the calendar is intended as a reference or for a more decorative purpose, they might want to select the **Banner** or **Jazz** style. Have them click **Next** to continue.

Calendar Wizard *(cont.)*

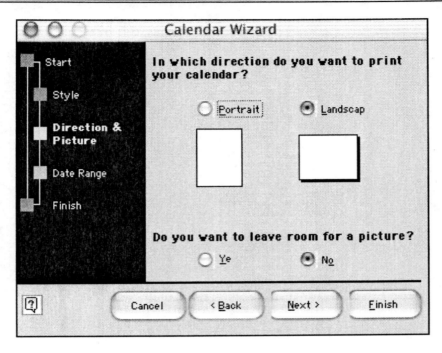

3. Have students select the direction in which they want their calendars to print, either Portrait (vertical) or Landscape (horizontal). Then they can decide if they want to leave room for a picture. Depending on the style and direction they have selected, they might find a picture takes up too much room. Have them click **Next** to continue.

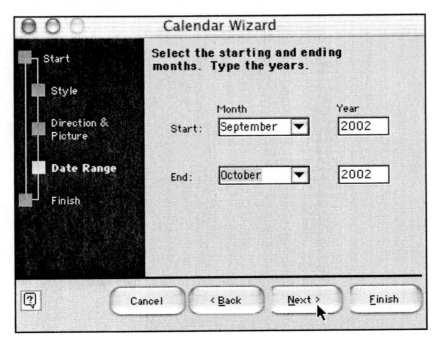

4. Have students select the starting and ending dates of their calendars. Make sure that they enter the years in the boxes provided. Have them click **Next** to continue.

Calendar Wizard *(cont.)*

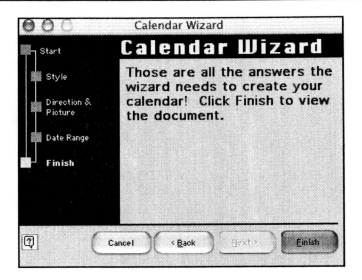

5. The calendar is ready for students to view! Have them click **Finish** to exit the Wizard and see their personalized calendars.

6. If there is anything that students want to change about their calendars, or if they want to use a different style than the one they chose, they can simply open the Calendar Wizard and start again.

Tips and Tricks

- Students can change the graphic that the template automatically adds to the calendar and replace it with a graphic that is specific to a season or holiday, or even a graphic that represents their school. To do this, make sure that they chose the option to leave room for a picture in Step 3. If they did not, they can open the Calendar Wizard again and start over.

  Have students click the existing picture. They can then go to the **Insert** menu and select **Picture**. If they want to use the Microsoft Clip Gallery, have them select **Clip Art**. If they want to use a graphic that they have in their files, have them select **From File**.

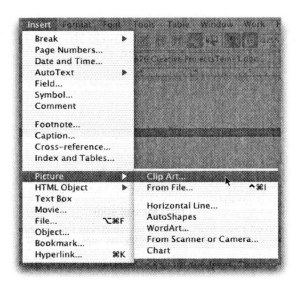

Calendar Wizard *(cont.)*

If they are using the Clip Gallery, they can scroll through the categories to find an appropriate graphic, click the selected graphic, and click **Insert**.

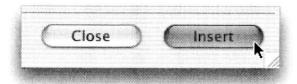

The new graphic will appear in the space provided by the calendar.

- Students could also use WordArt to personalize their calendars. Before doing this, once again make sure that students chose the option to leave room for a picture in Step 3. If they did not, they can open the Calendar Wizard again and start over.

Have students select the Insert WordArt button from the Drawing toolbar. If they do not see the Drawing toolbar, have them go to the **View** menu, select **Toolbars**, and select **Drawing**.

Students can then select a WordArt Style and click **OK**. Then they can type their names into the dialog box and press **OK**. When the WordArt appears on the page, they can use the grabber handles to fit it in the space provided.

Note: It might be necessary to delete the existing text box before adding WordArt and a graphic to the page.

Change Game

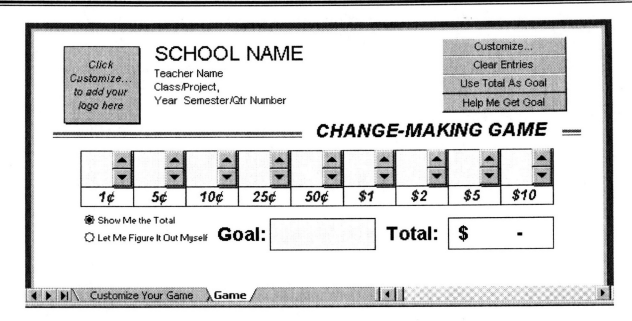

Software Application

Microsoft Excel

Using the Template

1. To customize the header on the game page, select **Customize Your Game** located in the bottom left hand corner of the template. Type your school and class information into the labeled text boxes. To include a logo, choose **Select Logo** and go to the location where your logo is stored. Highlight the logo's file name and select **Insert**. The Change Game template will automatically resize and place your logo. Select **Lock and Save Sheet** to save this information permanently to your template. If this button is not selected, the information will only be available for this game.

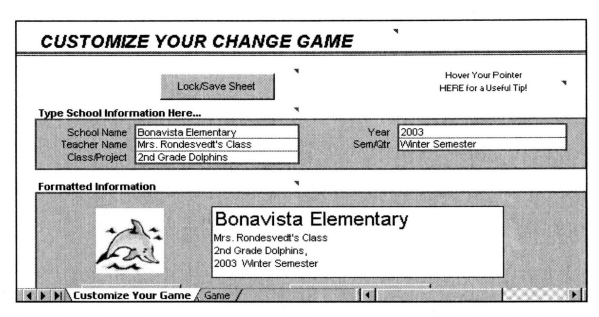

Change Game *(cont.)*

2. To play the game, students can select either **Show Me the Total** or **Let Me Figure It Out Myself**.

   If students select **Show Me the Total**, the total money value is displayed as students make various coin choices. The value moves up and down as coins are added or taken away.

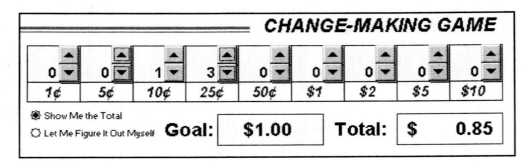

   If students select **Let Me Figure It Out**, the total is not displayed as students make coin choices. In order for them student to check their responses, students must select **Show Me the Total** when they assume that the total is correct.

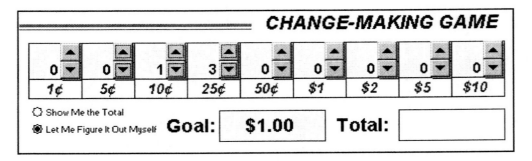

3. Make sure that students do not type any values in the **Total:** cell. This cell has a formula in it that is used to calculate the total value of the change selected. The formula will not work if the cell is changed. If students accidentally type a number into this cell, have them go to **Edit** on the Menu Bar and select **Undo Typing** to remove the number and return the cell to its original formula. Simply deleting the value added by mistake will not restore the formula to the cell.

Change Game *(cont.)*

4. Select the **Use Total as Goal** button if students will benefit from seeing the total change as they add or remove change.

Bonavista Elementary

Mrs. Rondesvedt's Class
2nd Grade Dolphins,
2003 Winter Semester

Customize...
Clear Entries
Use Total As Goal
Help Me Get Goal

CHANGE-MAKING GAME

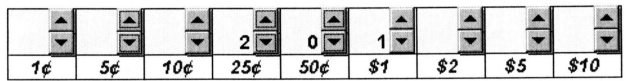

1¢	5¢	10¢	25¢	50¢	$1	$2	$5	$10
			2	0	1			

● Show Me the Total
○ Let Me Figure It Out Myself **Goal:** $0.00   **Total:** $ 1.50

5. Select the **Help Me Get My Goal** button if students will benefit from being shown the most common change choice. An unlimited quantity of each type of change is assumed.

Bonavista Elementary

Mrs. Rondesvedt's Class
2nd Grade Dolphins,
2003 Winter Semester

Customize...
Clear Entries
Use Total As Goal
Help Me Get Goal

CHANGE-MAKING GAME

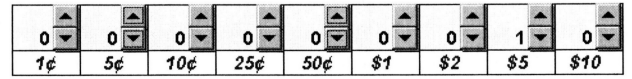

1¢	5¢	10¢	25¢	50¢	$1	$2	$5	$10
0	0	0	0	0	0	0	1	0

● Show Me the Total
○ Let Me Figure It Out Myself **Goal:** $5.00   **Total:** $ 5.00

Change Game *(cont.)*

Extension Ideas

- **At Home Practice**: Send home a copy of The Change Making Game on a floppy or e-mail it home for students who have computers with *Microsoft Excel*. Include instructions. Give parameters for the Goal and a number of problems that are to be solved. Have students print their game results—The Goal, Total and Change Selected—for each problem. For those students who do not have computers at home, print several examples with the goal quantity entered and the change section choices left blank. Instruct these students to write the number of coins needed from each section to make the goal. Have students share their solutions with others in the class in a game-like fashion by having them challenge others to solve their problem with different change choices.

- **Speed Challenges**: Have students see how quickly they can solve a particular problem or change goal. Make sure to make the challenges fair so that students of equal ability can compete with each other and have an equal chance to win.

- **Skill Building Activity**: Challenge students to see how many change problems they can complete in one minute. Then, challenge them to see if they can increase their score over time. For example: if a student starts out being able to solve three change problems in one minute, challenge the student to see if it is possible to able to solve six change problems in a minute. Make sure each student works from his/her base and has help in selecting a realistic goal.

- **Teacher-made Word Problems**: Create word problems that require making change a part of the solution. Print the word problems on cards using *Microsoft Word* and distribute them to the students. Have the students use The Change Game to help solve the problem. **Trick:** Make the cards by creating six or eight equally sized text boxes in a *Word* document. Enter a word problem in each box. When all boxes are filled, print and then cut them apart.

- **Student-made Word Problems**: Another alternative to this concept is to have the students use The Change Game to create word problems for other students to solve. Have the student print the word problem on a card and verify the answer using The Change Game.

Chart It!

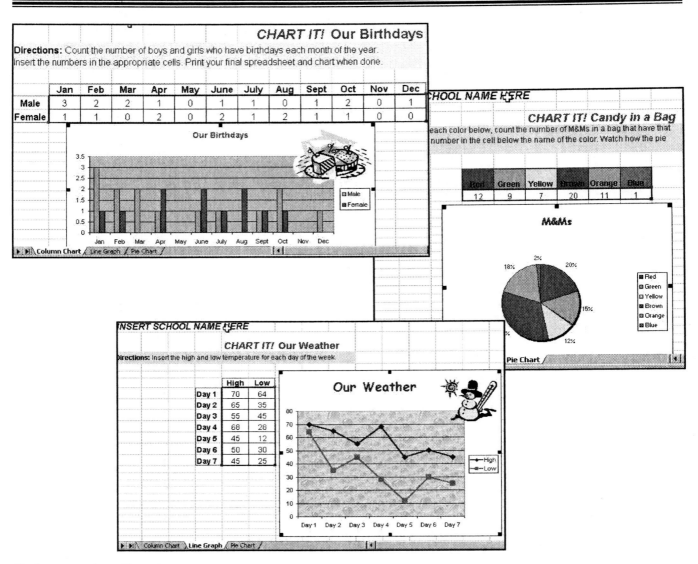

Software Application

Microsoft Excel

Using the Template

1. The **Chart It!** Template includes three separate worksheets—Column Chart, Line Graph, and Pie Chart. Have students click on the tabs at the bottom of the workbook to select a worksheet.

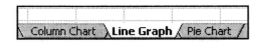

2. The **Column** worksheet has a chart that has been created to show class birthdays. Select the cell (A1) that reads **INSERT SCHOOL NAME HERE**. Type in the header information for your class.

Chart It! *(cont.)*

3. Have students follow the directions given in the yellow box. (**Directions:** Count the number of boys and girls who have birthdays each month of the year. Insert the numbers in the appropriate cells.)

   Delete the directions in the yellow box before printing by going to the **Edit** menu and selecting **Clear** and then **All**. Print your final spreadsheet and chart when complete.

4. With the Line Graph worksheet, your students can keep track of a week's worth of weather. Click the tab to select this chart. Select the cell (A1) that reads **INSERT SCHOOL NAME HERE.** Type the header information you want to use to describe your class.

5. Have students follow the directions given in the yellow box. (**Directions:** Insert the high and low temperature for each day of the week.)

   Delete the directions in the yellow box before printing by going to the **Edit** menu and selecting **Clear** and then **All**. Print your final spreadsheet and chart when done.

6. If students want to change the color of the text, have them first select the text to be changed by clicking in the cell where the text begins. Have them look in the text entry line beside the = sign to check that all the text is selected.

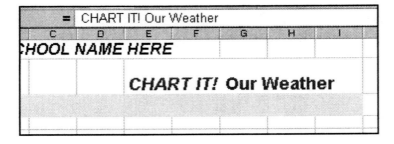

If all the text is selected, students can select the **Color Formatting** button, the letter **A**. Students can select the color visible or use the down triangle to make more color choices available. (If students are using *Microsoft Excel 2000/2001* or *XP/X*, have them select the **Font color** menu.)

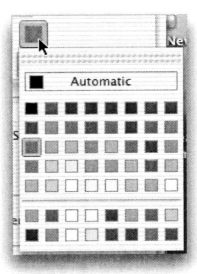

Chart It! *(cont.)*

7. To use the Pie Chart worksheet with your class, distribute a bag of small candies of assorted colors to the class. Students can make graphs of the number of candies of each color that can be found in a bag. Select the cell (A1) that reads **INSERT SCHOOL NAME HERE.** Type in the header information you want to use to describe your class.

Have students follow the directions given in the yellow box. Delete the directions before printing by going to the **Edit** menu and selecting **Clear** and then **All.** Print your final spreadsheet and chart when complete.

Tips and Tricks

- The templates are set up for very specific graphing and charting activities. It is not difficult to alter the format to accommodate other themes. For example, the Pie Chart could be changed to chart costume choices for Halloween.

1. If the tabs are not showing at the bottom of the screen for the chart or graph type, go to **Window** on the **Menu Bar** and down to **Arrange.** Make sure **Horizontal** and **Windows of Active Work Book** is selected. To change the name information bar, go to cell A1 and type in your class information.

2. Decide on the number of categories necessary for the chart. For a pie graph, too many categories makes labeling the sections difficult. There are six categories in the template. To keep it simple the first time, use six categories.

3. To Change the size of the categories, if there is not enough space for the label, highlight the columns F through K, and then move your cursor over the line between the letters until the left-right arrows are showing. Hold the mouse button down and drag the column marker to the size needed. With all the columns highlighted, all the columns will change together.

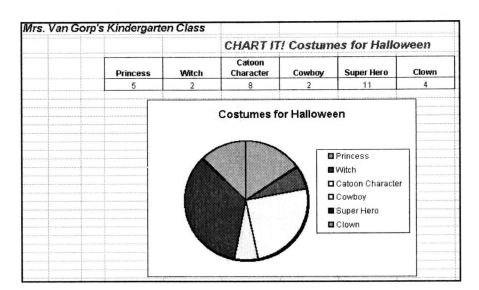

Mrs. Van Gorp's Kindergarten Class						
		CHART IT! Costumes for Halloween				
	Princess	Witch	Catoon Character	Cowboy	Super Hero	Clown
	5	2	8	2	11	4

Costumes for Halloween

- Princess
- Witch
- Catoon Character
- Cowboy
- Super Hero
- Clown

Chart It! *(cont.)*

4. Have students enter the numbers for each new category choice and the pie chart will change accordingly.

5. To create a different chart using the same data, select the **Chart Wizard** tool. The select the type of graph: bar, line, pie for example. The Chart Wizard will guide you through the process of making the graph or chart.

6. It is important to choose where the graph or chart will be placed. If it is to be on the same page as the pie chart select **As Object in Pie Chart** or if it is to be separate, select **As New Sheet**.

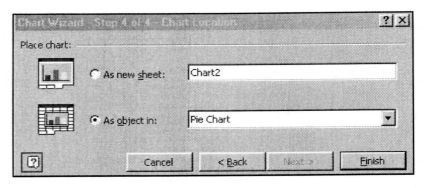

7. To move the new bar graph, click inside the graph in a white area and drag it to its new location. If you want to change the size of the graph, select one of its corners and pull it larger or smaller, as needed. The pie graph will remain on the sheet so it will either need to be covered up by the new graph or moved so the two can be seen separately.

The chart below shows both a bar and pie chart while the chart on the right shows only a bar graph. The two graphs below were moved so that they would both be visible. The chart on the right has the bar graph covering the pie graph.

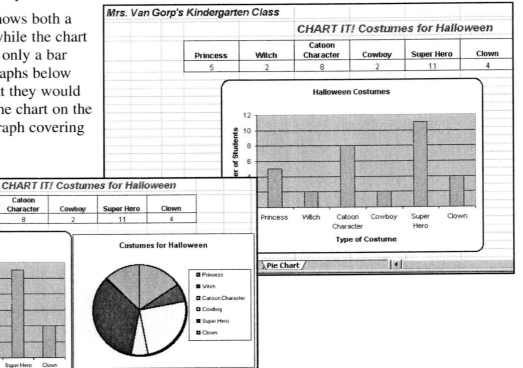

Chart It! *(cont.)*

Extension Ideas

- **Classroom Favorite Surveys**: Have each student select a topic that lends itself to surveying. Topic ideas might include:

    What is your favorite ice cream? Chocolate, Vanilla, Strawberry, Cookies and Cream

    What is your favorite movie? Monsters, Inc., Scooby Doo, Stuart Little 2, Toy Story 2

    What is your favorite fast food restaurant? McDonalds, Burger King, Wendy's, Taco Bell

- **Graphing Classroom Activities**: As your class participates in activities, have them brainstorm ideas for graphing. Topics might include:

    What are you for the Thanksgiving feast? A Native American or a Pilgrim

    What Cross Country Field Day activity are you doing? High Jump, Relay, 50-Yard Dash

- **Curriculum Related Graphs and Charts**: Any curriculum area that has number references that can be compared provide great material for charts and graphs:

    Social Studies: Number of Soldier and Civilians Killed During World War II for Each Fighting Nation

    Science: Weather Data from Different Locations for a Given Time Period

    (Temperature, Moisture, Wind)

    Language Arts: Number of Books Written by Different Children's Authors

    Music: Number of Beats per Measure—Tempo—for Different Styles of Music

    (March, Fox Trot, Waltz)

    Economics: Comparison of Daily Prices for Stocks and Bonds for a Defined Period of Time

Country Report

Software Application

Microsoft PowerPoint

Using the Template

1. The Country Report template has ten slides—title, location, geographic features, climate, environment, history, customs and traditions, government, economy, and tourism. Scroll down to access all the slides.

2. Have students replace the **Name of Your Country** text with their country's name. Have them add their name, the teacher's name, and the grade.

3. Have students scroll to the second slide, the location slide. Direct them to replace the **(your country)** text with the name of the country. If desired, they can use the **Find and Replace** feature of *PowerPoint* to replace this information throughout the presentation. Have them go to the **Edit** menu and select **Replace**. In the dialog box that appears, they can type (your country)—including the parentheses—in the **Find:** box and the name of the country in the **Replace with:** box.

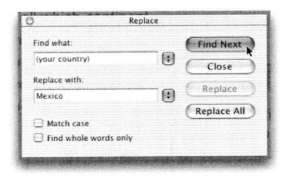

Have them select **Find Next** if they want to replace the text one instance at a time. Have them select **Replace All** to replace every instance of the text in the document.

Country Report *(cont.)*

4. Have students select the paragraph on the slide and type information about the continent on which the country is located and any nearby countries that border it. If students type more information than the text box can hold, *PowerPoint* will automatically adjust the text to fit it.

5. Have students add a graphic of a map showing their country. To look for a graphic in the Microsoft Clip Gallery, they can double click in the **Double click to add clip art** section. This will open the Clip Gallery. Have them try looking under the Maps category. If they do not see a map of the country there, have them type the name of the country into the **Search:** box and press the **Search** button to try to find more clip art.

   If students have a graphic of a map in their files, have them go to the **Insert** menu and select **Picture**, then **From File**. Have them navigate to find the graphic and click **Insert** to add it to the slide. When the graphic appears on the slide, students can use the mouse to move it to the box which reads **Double click to add clip art**. It will automatically be formatted to fit in the space.

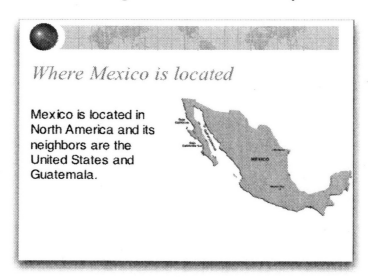

6. Have students use the instructions for steps 3, 4, and 5 to complete the remaining slides.

Country Report *(cont.)*

Tips and Tricks

- Students can add excitement to their *PowerPoint* presentations by adding movies. For example, if they were creating a presentation about Mexico, they could add a movie of a hurricane to a description of the tropical climate.

  To add a movie to a slide, students can go to the **Insert** menu and select **Movies and Sounds**. They can select **Movie from Gallery** (the Microsoft Clip Gallery) or **Movie from File**.

  Have students navigate to the movie and press **Insert** to add it to the slide. A dialog box will appear asking if you want the movie to play automatically during a slide show. Students can click **Yes** to have the movie play automatically and **No** if they want the movie to play only when clicked with the mouse.

  Once the movie has been added, students can grab it with the mouse and move it to the **Double click to add clip art** box. *PowerPoint* will automatically format it in the space provided.

If students want to make any changes to the way the movie plays, they can go to the **Slide Show** menu, select **Animation**, and select **Custom**. In the dialog box that appears, they can click the **Options** tab and select **Play Using Animation Order**. Then they can click the **Order and Timing** tab and change the animation options under **Start animation**.

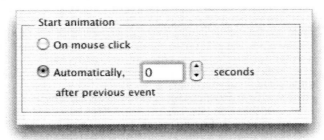

Extension Idea

- Students can modify the template to create state or province reports.

Cryptogram

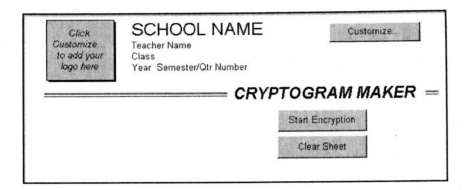

Software Application

Microsoft Excel

Using the Template

1. The cryptogram template is a *Microsoft Excel* program that allows you to create a custom cryptogram or secret message. To customize the header on this template, select the **Customize** button located in the top right hand corner of the template. Type in your school and class information and include a logo. If you choose **Lock and Save Template,** this information will be saved in a permanent way to your template. If you choose, **Lock but Don't Save**, the information will be kept for the duration of your cryptogram creation, but it will not change the template.

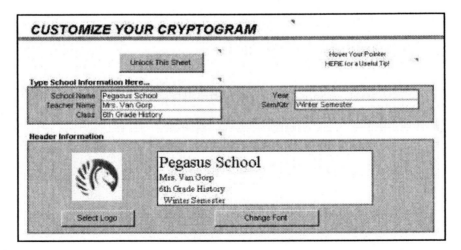

   The red arrows in the Customize section indicate that comments have been added to some of the cells. The comments provide additional tips for customizing the worksheet. Move your mouse over the cells with the red arrows to view the comments.

2. The Cryptogram Template has two worksheets—Cryptogram and Key. Show students how to use the tabs to access the different worksheets.

Cryptogram *(cont.)*

3. Students will need to add a key so that the letters of their messages have an encrypted value. Have them select the **Key** tab at the bottom of the template. Then they can type in the original letters and their corresponding encrypted values.

Original Encrypted Value

A	O
B	Q
C	B
D	C
E	U
F	J

4. When students have finished, show them how to return to the Cryptogram section of the template by selecting **Cryptogram** at the bottom of the template.

5. To create their cryptograms, students should select **Start Encryption** and type the message in the dialog box that appears.

6. After writing the message, students should select the **OK** button. The cryptogram will be displayed on the template page.

7. At this point, the cryptogram can be saved and/or printed out. When the cryptogram is printed, it will be personalized with the information that was added and ready for student use.

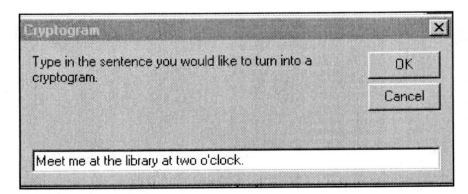

Cryptogram *(cont.)*

Extension Ideas

The American Heritage Dictionary defines a *Cryptogram* as "a piece of writing in code." In essence, it is a secret message. Cryptograms have long been an included activity in many newspapers, enjoyed by those wanting a challenge and a diversion. Its relevance in education has long been debated. Some feel the activity has worth and others feel it is only a time-filler. Relevant uses of this activity might include the following activities:

- Teachers can send students a positive or motivational secret message.

- Teachers can provide students with an activity to help them remember something important like a famous quote, where the process of solving the cryptogram will help them remember the information. For example: John F. Kennedy's Inaugural Address: "…ask not what your country can do for you. Ask what you can do for your country."

- Students can challenge other students to solve their encrypted message as a problem-solving, game-like activity.

- Teachers can relate the secret message activity to real life historical situations that have included secret messages like spy missions during World War II and other artificial intelligence projects.

- Students can create challenges for their parents to complete at home to encourage students and parents to work together.

- Classes can create a school-wide challenge to discover the mystery, secret message slogan chosen for each class.

- Parents, teachers and or students can create a challenge for a theme day or game at an in-school party.

"Don't Miss It!" Posters

Software Application

Microsoft Word

Modifying the Template

1. "Don't Miss It!" posters are perfect for your class events or fundraisers. There are five posters available in the template—Get on Target, Parent-Teacher Night, Yard Sale, Book Sale, and Annual Car Wash. Scroll down to view all the templates.

2. To have students personalize the "Don't Miss It—Get on Target" template by adding the date and location of the event, have them click inside the text box at the right-hand side of the document. They can select the word "date" and the symbols around it and type the date of the event.

3. To personalize the remaining templates, students can click inside the textbox that appears under the graphic and select the **Insert School Name Here** text. They can type the name of their school, then click the lines underneath and type the location and time of the event. Students may need to change the font size, color, or style to make it more suitable for the poster.

4. If possible, print the poster in color.

"Don't Miss It" Posters

Tips and Tricks

- If you have trouble moving the picture, you may need to format it differently. Click the picture to select it. Go to the **Format** menu and select **Picture**. If you are using *Word 97* or *98*, go to the **Position** tab and select **Float Over Text**. (This isn't necessary for subsequent versions of *Word*.) Then you can select how you would like the text to wrap around the picture.

Extension Idea

- Students can use the "Don't Miss It!" Posters template to create research posters. Research posters are a great method for students, especially younger students, to display information that they have learned.

  Have students use one of the simpler templates, such as the Yard Sale template. (The Don't Miss It—Get on Target!" template might be more difficult to modify.) To change the title, have them click once on the title text. This will open the WordArt toolbar. Click **Edit Text** on the toolbar and type the new text in the dialog box that appears.

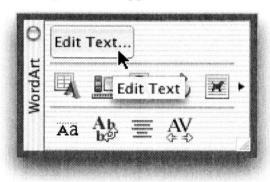

You can use the formatting buttons below the **Edit Text** button to change the style, color, or shape of the title.

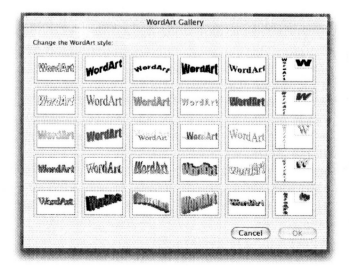

"Don't Miss It!" Posters *(cont.)*

Delete the graphic by clicking once on it and pressing the **backspace** or **delete** key. To add a new graphic, go to the **Insert** menu, select **Picture**, and then choose **Clip Art** to add art from the Microsoft Clip Gallery or **From File** to use a picture in your files.

Delete the text in the text box by selecting it and pressing **backspace** or **delete**. If any of the lines remain, click them once and press **backspace** or **delete** again. Add your new text. You may need to adjust the font size and style, the font color, or the alignment of the text.

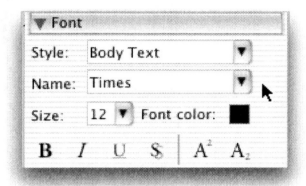 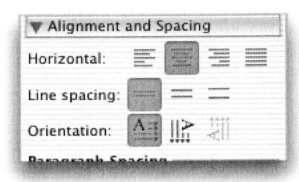

When the poster is finished, print it on a color printer, if possible, and display in the classroom.

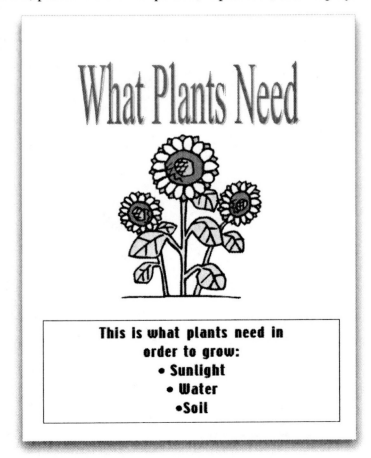

Fractions Graphing

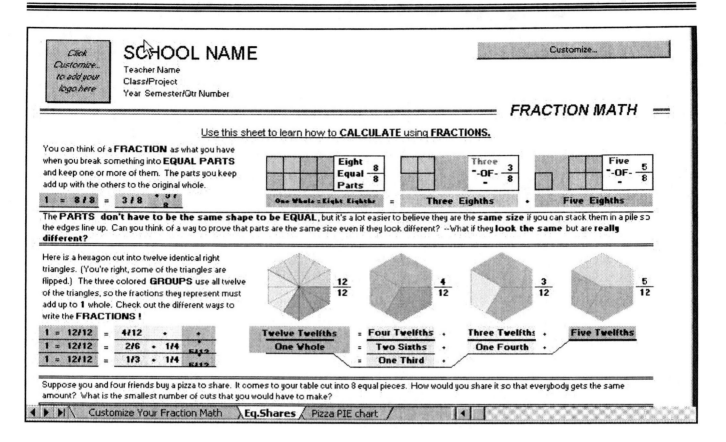

Software Application

Microsoft Excel

Using the Template

1. This template is designed to help students see a graphic representation of fractions. It has an explanation of how fractions work as well as a calculation section.

2. Customize the name and class information by selecting the **Customize...** bar in the top right corner of the template. Then, type in the school information and add a logo. When finished, select **Eq. Shares** to go back to the main template.

3. The top portion of the template explains how fractions work. Students read the material and look at the graphics provided.

4. The bottom portion of the template provides a calculation area where values can be changed and graph results can be viewed. When the values have been selected, 8 pieces and 4 people...**Do the PIZZA Pie Chart** or **PIZZA Pie chart (The Easy Way)** can be selected to view each chart.

Fractions Graphing *(cont.)*

Do the Pizza Pie Chart

Shows 8 slices

Each divided into 4 pieces...

1 for each person, 8 times

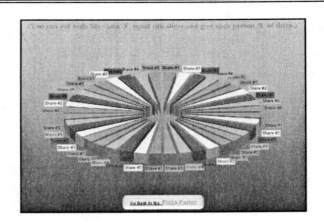

Pizza Pie chart

(The Easy Way)

Shows 8 slices

2 for each person

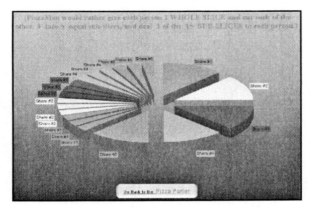

5. Changing the values will produce different fractions and different pie results. Have students vary the number of slices and number people and predict, and then see, the outcome.

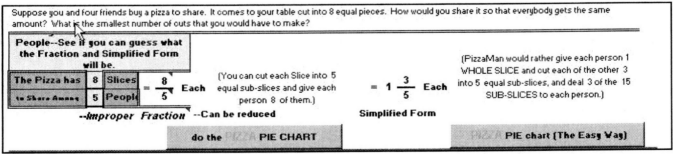

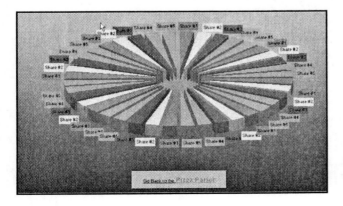

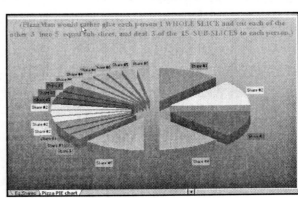

Graph Paper

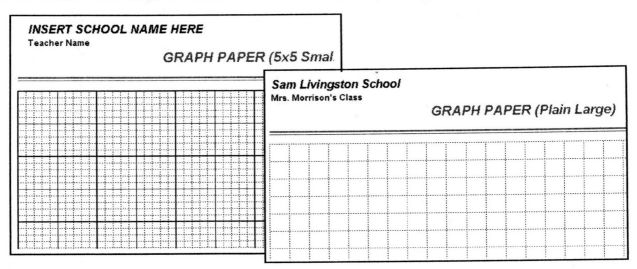

Software Application

Microsoft Excel

Using the Template

1. There are five graph paper types and sizes to choose from when using this template. Show students how to select the type by clicking on its tab at the bottom left of the template window. **Plain** is selected for this example.

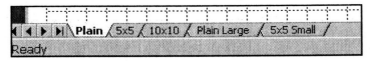

2. To fill a cell with color, students should select the cell or cells first. Then they can select the **Paint Can** on the **Formatting** button bar. If the color showing at the bottom of the paint can is not the desired color or if they wish to remove the color from the cell or cells, have them click the arrow to the right of the can. This will open the paint pallet. Students can choose another color or select **No Fill** if no color is desired.

3. To select a border for a cell, remove the border, or change the cell border in some way, first select the cell or cells. Then, select the **Borders Button** on the Formatting button bar. The one shown here would put a dark border around the outside of the cell or cells selected.

There are other choices, too, including no border, or borders on specific sides of the cell. To take the cell lines off the design, select the cell border that has no edges.

 Border on all the edges of the cells selected.

 No border on any of the cells selected.

 Border on the bottom edge of the cells selected.

Graph Paper *(cont.)*

4. Coloring in the squares by using several different border choices formed the designs below. The example on the left shows a quilt square and a face design.

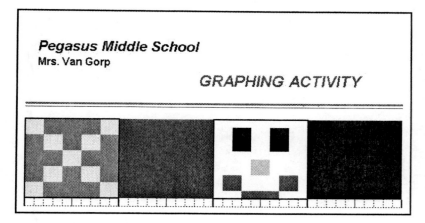

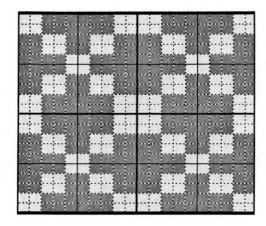

Extension Activities

- **Math Coordinate Designs**: Patterns on graph paper can be creative endeavors where the mathematics of the design or the relationship between the different cells is not considered. However, there is also some math involved in a design or pattern. The graph paper can be set up with the cell reference points showing, so that when the reference points are given as instructions, a pattern can be created. Working with this technique can help students understand coordinates and how to use coordinates on a grid.

To have the row and column markers showing on the graph paper, select **Tools** . . . **Options** . . . **View** and then select **Row & column headers.** With these markers showing, a location can be designated. The cell that is colored is D6. To instruct someone to color the next cell to the right with the markers would be to call the cell E6. The cell below would be D7 and the one to the right of that would be E7. If all those cells were colored, the result would be the pattern on the right.

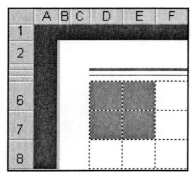

Students can be challenged to create a design given cell markers.

For example:

   Red: D6, E6, D7, D8, F9, F10, G9, G10

   Blue: D8, E8, F8, G8

   Take off all cell borders for the square (D-G, 6-10)

   Select a solid border for the outside if the square (D-G, 6-10)

Creative Art Designs: Have students select one of the graph paper sizes. Direct them to think of a design that can be made using squares. Their design can be a quilt with repeated patterns, simulation of a view in nature, or a manufactured item like a car or a house. Have students create a frame around their design and print it out when finished. Create a bulletin board. The results will be stunning!

Hangman

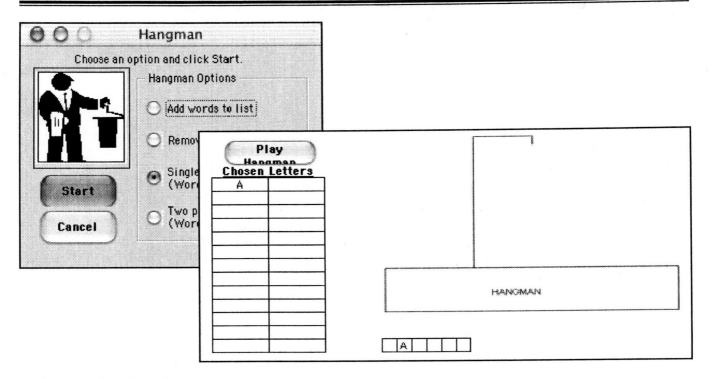

Software Application

Microsoft Excel

Using the Template

1. The Hangman template gives your students the opportunity to play an actual game of "Hangman" with *Microsoft Excel*. When you open the Hangman template, you are presented with the option of having students use the list of words provided by the template, adding your own words, or having students play a two-person game in which one player enters the words and the other tries to solve the puzzle.

2. If you choose to add your own words, select the button beside the first option, **Add words to list**, and click on the **Start** button. A dialog box will open. Type the first word you wish to add.

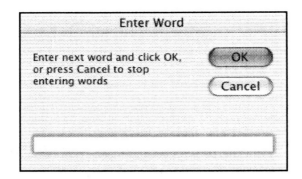

Click the **OK** button after each word. Click **Cancel** to stop entering words and return to the first dialog box.

Hangman *(cont.)*

3. To start the game with one player, select the **Single Player Game** option. The game will appear and a dialog box will prompt a student for his or her first guess.

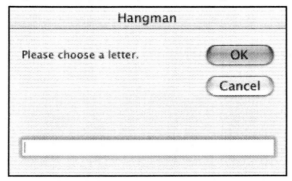

4. A correct guess will add the letter to the puzzle. An incorrect guess will add a body part to the tower.

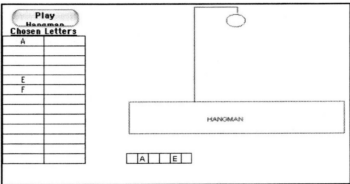

5. When the puzzle has been solved, or the entire hangman has been drawn, the game is over.

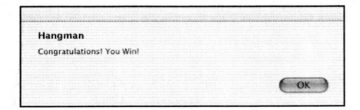

6. To have students play a two-player game, select the **Two Player Game** option. Have the first student type into the dialog box a word for the second student to guess and click **OK**.

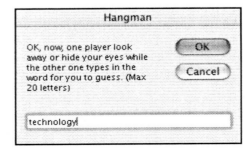

7. The second student will play the hangman game just like a one-player game.

Hangman *(cont.)*

Tips and Tricks

- When you open the Hangman file, you may get a message that the file you are opening contains macros. Click on **Enable Macros**. This template will not work correctly if macros are not enabled.

Extension Ideas

This template's value lies in its ability to be personalized. Hangman games reinforce a student's memory for letter placement, letter combinations, and spelling patterns. The student is able to think of how words work when guessing possible letters. A strategy for example might be to guess the vowels in the word first. Another strategy might be to try to find word family combinations like *-ing* or *-ell* that might exist in the word.

For the student to gain more than just the value of playing a thinking game, the teacher must carefully select the content that is to be used.

- Use the **Add Words to List** option to add your weekly spelling or vocabulary words to the list. You may want to select the **Remove all words from list** option first. If students have a familiarity with the words being studied, adding a hangman game helps to build visual memory for the words. Before beginning the game, students can brainstorm phonic rules that relate to the words, irregular spelling examples contained in the words, and other clues about the words that might help them solve the word puzzle quickly.
- Try a Hangman Competition as one component of a Problem Solving Games Day. Teachers and/or students could generate the puzzles and then students could rotate through the event center to see how many successful Hangman games they could play with in a certain time frame like 15 minutes. Another scoring alternative might be to award points for solution speed and accuracy.
- Have students share Hangman challenges with their families. Encourage students to create word lists appropriate for different members of their family: simple word lists for a younger sibling, difficult lists for an older sibling and special challenges for parents. Students can have fun thinking up gimmicks for the word lists they create. The game can be taken home on a floppy disk or e-mailed to students' homes as an attachment.

Homework Recordkeeping

INSERT NAME OF SCHOOL HERE

Student Name _____

HOMEWORK ASSIGNMENT SHEET

MONTH: _____

Week of:	Monday	Tuesday	Wednesday	Thursday	Friday

Insert Name of School Here

HOMEWORK CHART

This is a record of homework by _____

Date	Description	Completed	Attempted	Not Accepted	Redone
Totals	Total Number of Assignments = _____	× 5 pts = ___	× 3 pts = ___	× 0 pts = ___	× 2 pts = ___

Steps to compute your homework grade:
1. Calculate the total points for home completed, attempted, not accepted, and/or redone.
2. Add the total points for completed, not accepted, and/or redone homework. This is your Total Points Achieved.
3. Add the total number of assignments and multiply by 5 points. This equals the Total Possible Points.
4. Divide the Total Points Achieved by the Total Possible Points and multiply by 100. This is your Final Homework Grade.

Software Application

Microsoft Excel

Using the Template

1. The Homework Recordkeeping template allows students to keep personal records of their homework assignments. The template has two worksheets—Homework Chart and Assignment Sheet. Show students how to access the worksheets by clicking the tabs at the bottom of the workbook page.

2. Have students select the **Insert School Name Here** text and replace it by typing the name of their school.

3. Print the Homework Assignment sheet each week and have students add their names. They can use this sheet to write down their daily homework assignments.

4. Have students create their Homework Charts. They can begin by adding their names to the **This is a record of homework by** line. To make any changes, they will need to double-click in cell B3, where the text begins. Have them select the line after the word "by" and replace it with their names.

Homework Recordkeeping *(cont.)*

5. Have students click in cell B6 and type the date of the first assignment.

6. Have students click in cell C6 and type a description of the assignment.

7. If students have completed the assignment, have them add an "X" or another kind of marker in cell D6, under the **Completed** category. If students attempted the assignment, but didn't complete it, have them add a marker in cell E6, under the **Attempted** category. If the homework was turned in but not accepted, have them add a marker in cell F6, the **Not Accepted** category. If the homework was redone, have them mark in cell G6, the **Redone** category.

8. Have students repeat steps 5 through 8 for the remaining homework assignments.

9. When students have completed their assignments, have them add their totals at the last row of each column. They can add the total number of assignments at the end of the **Description** category, and then add the individual assignments for the final homework score in each category.

Tips and Tricks

- If students need more room to write their assignments on the Homework Assignment sheet, they can increase the row or column sizes. Have them move the mouse to the line that separates two columns or rows, click the mouse, and drag to increase the size.

- To make sure that the Homework Assignment sheet prints on only one page, go to the **View** menu and select **Page Break Preview**. This will open the worksheet in a new window, making it possible for you to see where the page breaks are in the document. To adjust the placement of the page breaks, click the dashed line. When you see the double-headed arrow, move the mouse until the entire document appears on page 1.

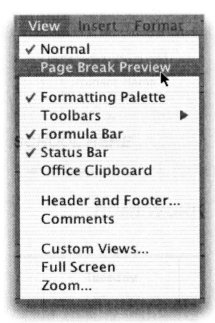

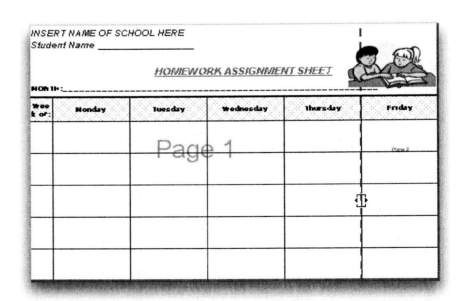

Lab Sheets

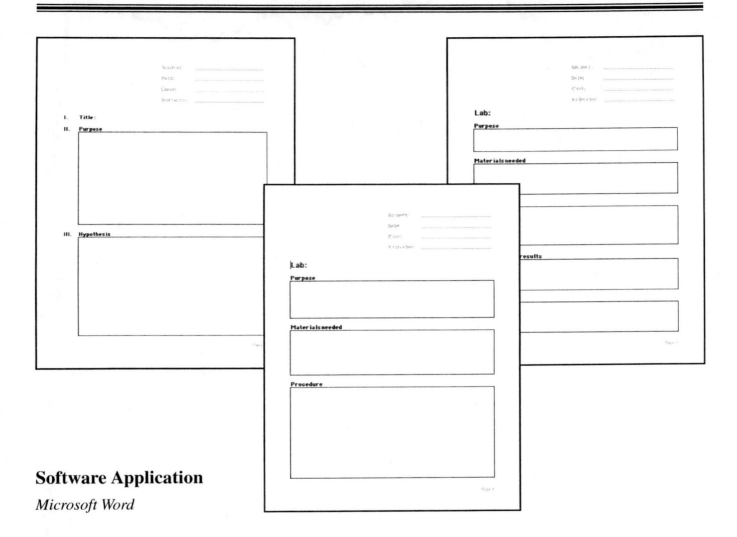

Software Application

Microsoft Word

Using the Template

1. When you open the Lab Sheets template, a dialog box will appear. Select the type of lab report you wish to create—Full, Short (1-page), or Short (2-page). (The Full Report has space for Purpose, Hypothesis, Procedure, Data/calculations/results, Conclusions, and Error Analysis. The Short Reports have space for Purpose, Materials Needed, Procedure, Observations/results, and Conclusions.) Click **OK** to continue.

Lab Sheets *(cont.)*

2. The top section of the sheet with the Date, Class, and Instructor information appears in gray, indicating that it is a header. To Change the text, go to the **View** menu and select **Header and Footer**.

The text will appear in a box with dashed lines around it. The Header and Footer toolbar will appear below it. Make any changes necessary and return to the main document either by going to **View—>Header and Footer** again or clicking the **Close** button on the Header and Footer toolbar.

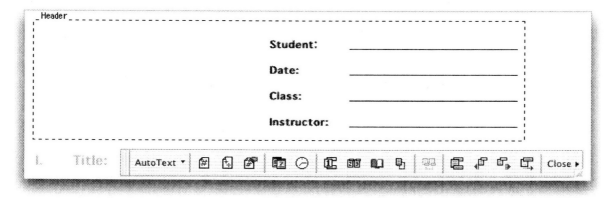

3. You can either print the page or have students fill it out as they complete their science experiment.

Tips and Tricks

- If you want to increase or decrease the amount of space in the boxes, first make sure that **Show/Hide All** is turned on. This option in the Standard toolbar allows you to see the non-printing characters such as tabs and paragraph marks that are usually invisible.

Lab Sheets *(cont.)*

Click the **Show/Hide All** button.

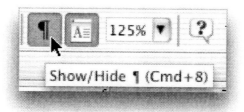

The arrows inside the boxes indicate line breaks, or soft returns. If you want to make a box smaller, delete some of these characters. If you want to make a box bigger, press **Shift + Enter** (Windows) or **Shift + Return** (Macintosh) to add additional line breaks. You may need to adjust the page breaks accordingly.

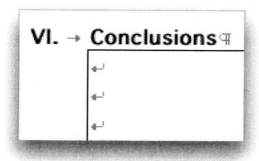

- If you want to add any additional boxes, select one of the boxes along with the line breaks inside of it. Go to the **Edit** menu and select **Copy**. Click the mouse where you want to add the additional box. Go to the **Edit** menu and select **Paste**.

Extension Idea

- Use this template to create storyboards, outlines for creative stories, or to plan information for book reports. Simply change the existing text to Characters, Setting, Plot, Events, and Resolution.

Lists and Charts

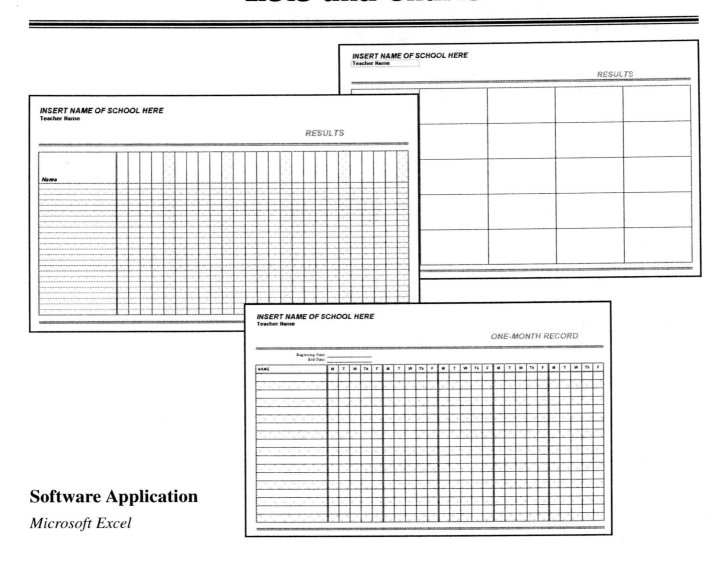

Software Application

Microsoft Excel

Using the Template

1. The Lists and Charts template consists of three worksheets—Vertical, Plain Grid, and One-Month Record. Have students use the tabs at the bottom of the page to select the worksheet they want to use.

2. Have students select the **Insert Name of School Here** and **Teacher Name** text and replace it with their school and teacher information.

3. For the One-Month Record template, have students type a beginning date and an ending date.

4. Students can either print the worksheet and write the information by hand, or enter the data directly onto the worksheet at the computer.

Lists and Charts *(cont.)*

Tips and Tricks

- If students are typing rows of numbers into the worksheet and need to add them, they can create formulas in *Excel* to automate the process. For example, if they were keeping track of their own progress while working on a research paper, they could use a formula to total what their scores were for each part of the project.

Have them click in the cell in which they want the total to appear.

Name		Notes	Outline	Rough Draft	Final Draft	Total
Brendan Carney		10	9	8	9	

The fastest method of having *Excel* add the results is to use the **AutoSum** button in the Standard toolbar. Click that button and *Excel* will guess the cells that you want to sum.

If *Excel* has chosen the correct cells, press Enter or Return to accept. The total will appear in the cell.

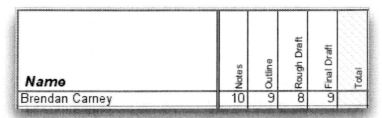

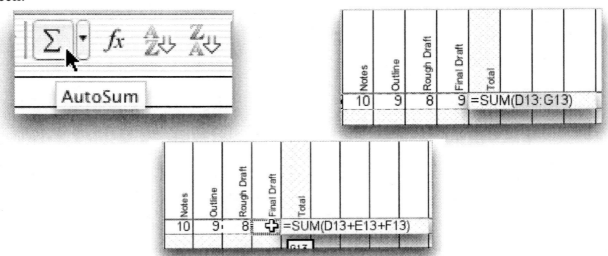

If *Excel* has not chosen the correct cells, students can click one by one in the cells they want to add, or click and drag over the selected cells. When the correct cells are included in the formula, they can press **Enter** or **Return** to accept.

Notes	Outline	Rough Draft	Final Draft	Total
10	9	8	9	36

Make Your Own Mini-Book

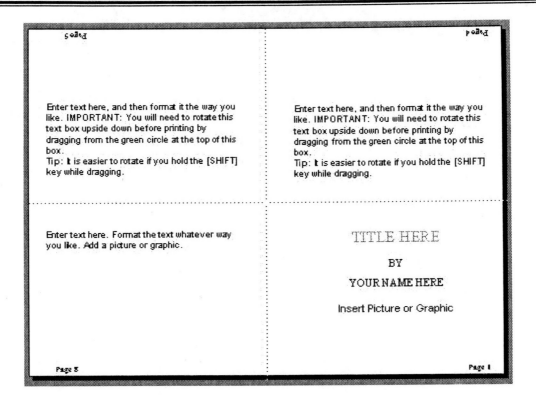

Software Application

Microsoft PowerPoint

Using the Template

1. Use this template with your students to create mini-books that are theme-, concept- or event-oriented. The book has eight pages created on two *PowerPoint* slides. The template guides the user on placement of the text and graphics for each of the eight pages.

2. Notice the page markers in each corner. Four of the page sections are right side up and four will need to be rotated half way around so they are upside down before printing. This is necessary to keep the page orientation correct when the pages are folded and cut after printing.

3. To have a successful project, it is important to plan the pages of the book, keeping in mind which text and pictures will appear side by side as the pages are opened. The cover page is by itself, as is the back page, while the other pages are in pairs, opening side-by-side.

Cover Page—Page 1 (Right Side Up)

Page 2 (Right Side Up) + **Page 3** (Up Side Down)

Page 4 (Up Side Down) + **Page 5** (Up Side Down)

Page 6 (Up Side Down) + **Page 7** (Right Side Up)

Back Page – Page 8 (Right Side Up)

Make Your Own Mini-Book *(cont.)*

4. A planning sheet can help students to focus on the content of their books before they begin work on the *PowerPoint* template. Have students brainstorm their ideas, write out their text, and look for graphics and photos. Have them lay out their material on a planning sheet like the one shown below.

Text:	**Cover Page/Front Page** (Right Side Up) Extras:	Photos:

Page 2 (Right Side Up)	**Page 3** (Up Side Down)

Page 4 (Up Side Down)	**Page 5** (Up Side Down)

Page 6 (Up Side Down)	**Page 7** (Right Side Up)

Text:	**Last Page/Back Page** (Right Side Up) Extras:	Photos:

Make Your Own Mini-Book *(cont.)*

5. Shown above is an example of what can be done with a mini-book. Note the right side up sections and the upside down sections. Photos are easiest added to the pages that stay right side up, as they will not rotate like the text will. To keep it simple, only put photos on the pages that do not need to be turned. (If photos are used on the upside down pages, they will need to be turned upside down in a paint program or a photo editing program, then saved before being inserted in the page section of the *PowerPoint* slide.) Encourage students to create distinctive front and back pages.

Make Your Own Mini-Book *(cont.)*

6. Show students how to enter text directly into the instruction box provided on each page.

   • **Highlight** the text that is in the template box.

   > Enter text here, and then format it the way you like. IMPORTANT: You will need to rotate this text box upside down before printing by dragging from the green circle at the top of this box.
   > Tip: It is easier to rotate if you hold the [SHIFT] key while dragging.

   • Press **backspace** or **delete** to remove the text.

   • Type the new text for the book in the blank box and format it.

   > **Our Class**
   > **Visit to the Zoo**
   > May 2002

   • Select the **Rotation tool** to turn the text. When selected, the text will be edged with four green handles.
   • Click on one of the handles and drag the text around until it is upside down.

7. Have students add a photo or graphic by selecting **Insert,** then **Picture**, and then the type and/or location of the image. They can move the image to a location on the mini page that fits the text. Coordinate their location and colors.

Make Your Own Mini-Book *(cont.)*

8. Printing the Mini-Book with card stock or another heavy weight paper is a good choice for this project. Only page two and page three of the modified template need to be printed. The first page is an instruction page. Print template page two first. Then, turn the paper so that page three of the template is correctly oriented with the side of the page just printed. How paper feeds through the printer will determine how the paper will be place in the printer tray for printing on the back side. Do a trial run, low print quality, in black/white and on regular paper to check the placement of the page for printing. When you have determined the orientation, make sure to change the properties of the printer to the highest print quality and heavy paper type, if that is an option. Then begin printing the final draft. Laminate the mini-book to protect it from excessive use, fold the pages, cut the tops and staple on the center fold. Enjoy sharing!

Extension Ideas

- **Class Field Trip Mini-Book**: Take photos during a field trip. Then have the photos developed and placed on a CD or have them scanned to digitize them. Include the photos and a description of the events on the pages of the mini-book.

- **All About Me**: Have students create an informational mini-book about significant events and people in their lives. They might include their birth, first steps, learning to ride a bike, a special vacation, school and recreational activities, and time with family members. Have them organize the content and decorate the pages with graphics and photos.

- **Mini-Book Report**: Students will enjoy the challenge of making a mini-book and representing the content of the book they are reviewing. Page content can include information about the author, the setting, the characters, the plot, and comments.

- **Moments in History**: Using this topic students can create a series of mini-books that relate to a topic in history. Important Moments in U.S. History, Greek Gods, Early Civilizations, Early Native American Societies, or Wars that Changed History are possible topic ideas.

- **Famous People Mini-Book Series**: By devoting one book to each famous individual, a series can be made for a particular theme. Create several different series like Famous Scientists, Famous Authors, Famous Politicians, Famous Sport Players, or Famous Movie Stars, and continue to add to a class collection.

Newsletter Wizard

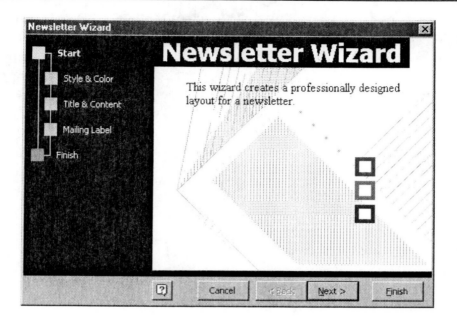

Software Application

Microsoft Word

Using the Template

1. The wizard asks for information before you begin entering the content of your newsletter. Once the information has been entered, the Newspaper Wizard will create a personalized title and several formatting options.

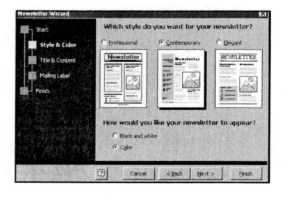

2. Have students click on **Next** to select the style of their newsletters. There are three style choices that can be made: professional, contemporary and elegant. The choice made will determine the layout, and positioning of the title and sections of the newsletter. The selection screen gives an idea of the differences. Students can also choose whether they want their newsletter to appear in color or black and white. While color is great, copying cost is often the reason for selecting black and white.

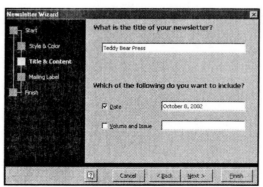

3. Have students click **Next** to move on to the Title, Date and Issue Options. Haves students add the title, date, and number of the issue. The wizard uses this information to create your newspaper template. Only the information that is desired needs to be entered. Sections can be left blank, if needed.

Newsletter *(cont.)*

4. Have students click **Next** to continue to the Mailing Label option. Students can click **Yes** if the newsletter will be mailed or **No** if it is not to be mailed. If the newsletter is to be mailed, the wizard will leave a space on the back blank so that a mailing label can be added.

5. Have students select **Finish** when all the choices have been made and the wizard will create a personalized template for them to use.

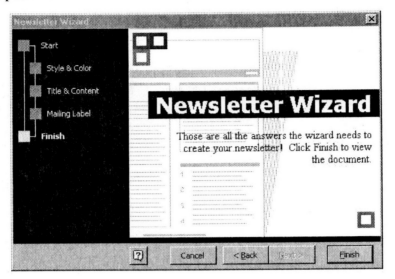

Below is a sample of a personalized Newsletter Template created with the Newsletter Wizard.

Newsletter *(cont.)*

6. The text that appears in the newly created newsletter has excellent instructions for using and changing the template. To keep these instructions in order to refer to them easily while working on the newsletter, have students choose **Print** from the **File** menu, select the appropriate printer settings, and then select **OK** or press **Enter** or **Return**.

7. Detailed instructions are given on the template for making the following changes:

   Formatting Text Boxes

   Using and Making Changes to Columns

   Inserting and Editing Pictures

   Personalizing the Mailing Section

   Continuing Articles across Pages

   Using Footers, Symbols and Borders

   Using and Changing Styles in the Template

8. As with other written projects, the content of the newsletter should be planned out before anything is added to the template. The type of newsletter will determine the content. If the newsletter focuses on upcoming events, the content will be different than if the newsletter focuses on providing information about a specific topic like choosing extra curricular activities. The information needs to be accurate, highlighted with pictures and/or graphics and it needs to have a creative, attention-getting style. Mapping out the content, as shown in the example below, is essential to putting together a good newsletter. Adaptations can be made to suit the newspaper style being used.

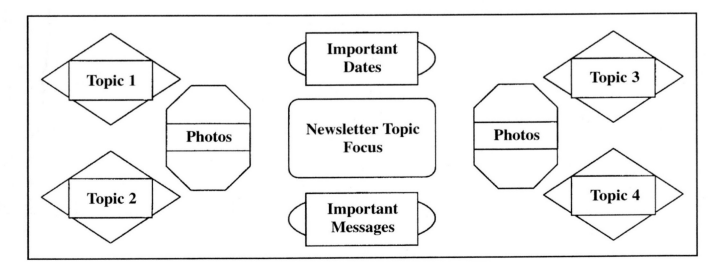

Newsletter *(cont.)*

Extension Ideas

- **Class Newsletter**: This basic theme allows the teacher and/or the students to report on the activities of the class. Content includes details of upcoming class events and reports on events that have already happened. Highlighting curriculum content, spotlighting individuals and providing links to community activities are other possible subjects.

- **Information Based Newsletter**: The newsletter format is a good one for covering controversial topics like Teen Drug Use, Smoking and Your Health, or Eating and Exercising for Your Body. Focusing on other topics of interest to students can produce great themes, too, such as After School Activities, Getting into Music, or Shopping for Fun and Savings.

- **Time in History**: Time period newspapers are great fun for students to make. The researching of historical articles and putting the information into a historical format helps put students into the time period mentally. The newsletter format can be used to present historically important information.

- **Science Fair Report**: There are always Science Fair projects that are well done, but the names of the winners and their project content is not always shared. A newsletter, highlighting preparations for the Science Fair, the results of competitions, and a focus on top projects is a great way to publicize this event. Be sure that photos are taken of the experience, of the winners and of the details of student presentations and displays. Don't forget to record the facts. Newspapers need to be accurate.

- **Website News**: Have a newsletter focus on subject-related websites. Different articles can highlight sites with different areas of focus. Some can relate to subject related material such as Science, Math, and Language Arts, while others can relate to technology related topics such as Safety on the Internet, Using the Internet, Tips and Tricks for *Microsoft Office*, Making a Movie Using Your Computer, or Computer Games. This newsletter format will provide a guide for students and parents to use while working on the Internet.

- **Entertainment News**: Don't forget the ever-popular joke and entertainment newsletter. Students love being funny and would have a great time writing and producing this style of newsletter.

Our Fifty States

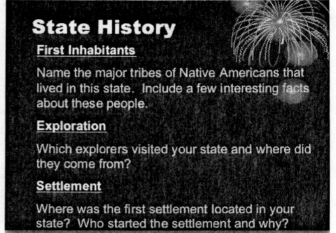
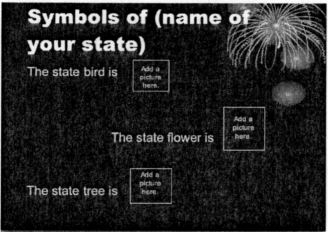

Software Application

Microsoft PowerPoint

Using the Template

1. The Our Fifty States template has 17 slides—Title, Symbols, State Nickname, State History (two slides), Statehood, Government, Maps, Population, Economy, Weather, Natural Resources (two slides), Places to Visit, Famous People, State Motto, and Works Cited. Scroll down to view all the slides.

2. Have students replace the **[Name of Your State]** text (including the brackets) with the state name. Have them add their names and the date.

3. Students can scroll to the next slide. They can replace the **(name of your state)** text (including the parentheses) with the state name. This slide has a note attached, which can be seen if students are using *Microsoft PowerPoint 2000/2001* or *XP/X*. If students are using *Microsoft PowerPoint 97/98*, they can go to the **View** menu and select **Notes Page** to view the notes. The notes page suggests that students use the Website 50States.com (**http://www.50States.com**) to find out more information about their state.

Our Fifty States *(cont.)*

4. After students have learned what their state bird, flower, and tree are, they can add graphics. To add graphics from their files, students can go to the **Insert** menu, select **Picture**, and choose **From File**. To add graphics from the Microsoft Clip Gallery, students can go to the **Insert** menu, select **Picture**, and choose **From File**.

5. Have students complete slides 3, 4, and 5 with information that they have found.

6. Have students continue to the sixth slide, **Statehood**. They can use the information they learned from their research to complete the blanks. Have them select each blank line and replace it with their own text. Have students do the same for the seventh slide, **Government**.

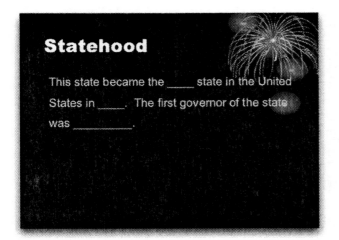
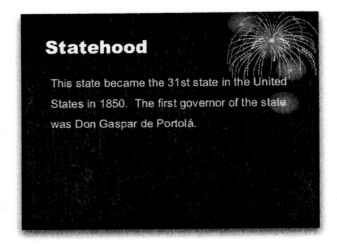

7. Have students scroll to the next slide, **Maps**. The instructions for this slide include a link to the Microsoft Digital Gallery Web site, where additional clip art and graphics can be found. If their computers are connected to the Internet, allow students to look for graphics on this site.

8. Have students scroll to the ninth slide, **Population**. The notes for this slide suggest that students use *Excel* to make a graph of the population information and import it into the slide show. To do this, have students open *Excel* and create their graphs. Then have them return to their slides, go to the **Insert** menu and, select **Chart**. This will open the Microsoft Graph application. Have students click the datasheet—not the sample graph—and then go to the **File** menu and select **Import File**.

Students can navigate to their *Excel* files and select their population graphs. After it has opened, students can quit the *Microsoft Graph* application and return to *PowerPoint*. The graph will be added to the slide.

Students could also use the *Microsoft Graph* application to create their population graphs.

Our Fifty States *(cont.)*

9. Have students use their research information to create the remaining slides, selecting and replacing text as needed.

Tips and Tricks

- If students cannot find the graphics that they need in the Microsoft Clip Gallery, they can search online for additional graphics. (Note: In order to download graphics, students need to use *Microsoft Office 2000/2001* or *XP/X*.) For example, if they need to find a graphic to represent the California state bird, the California Valley Quail, they could start their search by selecting the **Online** button in the Clip Gallery.

A dialog box will appear, asking if it is OK to launch the default browser. Have students click **Yes** if the computer is connected to the Internet. This will open the Microsoft Design Gallery.

Students could type the word "quail" into the **Search for:** box and press **Go**. The search results will appear in the window. To download any of the results to the Clip Gallery, select the download icon right under the graphic.

If your browser does not know how to save the file, the simplest way to add it to the Clip Gallery might be to have students save it to the desktop and return to the Clip Gallery again to import the graphic. Have them select the **Import** button and then navigate to the desktop to open the file. If students cannot click the file, they may need to click the **Show** pull-down menu and select **Design Gallery Live files** to have this type of file shown.

When the graphic has been imported, students can select it in the Clip Gallery and insert it into their presentations.

Periodic Table

Periodic Table of the Elements

This table is from Paul R. Frey, College Chemistry, 2nd ed. Copyright, 1958, by Prentice-Hall, Inc. --via College Outline Series FIRST-YEAR COLLEGE CHEMISTRY, Seventh Edition, 1951 (BARNES & NOBLE, Inc.) Reprinted, 1959 .... (amended 990217 to include more recently discovered and postulated elements- see "The Evolution of the Periodic System", Eric R. Scerri, Scientific American, September 1998, pp.78-83)

Light Metals — *Heavy Metals* — *Nonmetals*

Atomic Weight (★★★) / Element Name / Atomic (number)

Group	Ia	IIa	IIIb	IVb	Vb	VIb	VIIb	VIIIb			Ib	IIb	IIIa	IVa	Va	VIa	VIIa	VIIIa
1	H 1.008 / 1																	He 4.003 / 2
2	Li 6.94 / 3	Be 9.013 / 4											B 10.82 / 5	C 12.011 / 6	N 14.008 / 7	O 16 / 8	F 19 / 9	Ne 20.183 / 10
3	Na 22.991 / 11	Mg 24.32 / 12											Al 26.98 / 13	Si 28.09 / 14	P 30.975 / 15	S 32.066 / 16	Cl 35.457 / 17	A 39.944 / 18
4	K 39.1 / 19	Ca 40.08 / 20	Sc 44.96 / 21	Ti 47.9 / 22	V 50.95 / 23	Cr 52.01 / 24	Mn 54.94 / 25	Fe 55.85 / 26	Co 58.94 / 27	Ni 58.71 / 28	Cu 63.54 / 29	Zn 65.38 / 30	Ga 69.72 / 31	Ge 72.6 / 32	As 74.91 / 33	Se 78.96 / 34	Br 79.916 / 35	Kr 83.8 / 36
5	Rb 85.48 / 37	Sr 87.63 / 38	Y 88.92 / 39	Zr 91.22 / 40	Nb 92.91 / 41	Mo 95.95 / 42	Tc 99 / 43	Ru 101.1 / 44	Rh 102.91 / 45	Pd 106.4 / 46	Ag 107.88 / 47	Cd 112.41 / 48	In 114.82 / 49	Sn 118.7 / 50	Sb 121.76 / 51	Te 127.61 / 52	I 126.91 / 53	Xe 131.3 / 54
6	Cs 132.91 / 55	Ba 137.56 / 56	Lu 174.99 / 71	Hf 178.5 / 72	Ta 180.95 / 73	W 183.86 / 74	Re 186.22 / 75	Os 190.2 / 76	Ir 192.2 / 77	Pt 195.09 / 78	Au 197 / 79	Hg 200.61 / 80	Tl 204.39 / 81	Pb 207.21 / 82	Bi 209 / 83	Po 210 / 84	At (210) / 85	Rn (222) / 86
7	Fr (223) / 87	Ra 226.05 / 88	Lw (260) / 103	Rf (261) / 104	Db (262) / 105	Sg (263) / 106	Bh (262) / 107	Hs (265) / 108	Mt (266) / 109	* (269) / 110	* (272) / 111	* / 112	** / 113	** / 114	** / 115	** / 116	** / 117	** / 118

{★★★ Atomic Weights in parentheses indicate the weight of the most stable isotope}

** Elements not yet discovered

* Elements discovered but not yet officially named

Lanthanide Series	La 138.92 / 57	Ce 140.13 / 58	Pr 140.92 / 59	Nd 144.27 / 60	Pm 145 / 61	Sm 150.35 / 62	Eu 152 / 63	Gd 157.26 / 64	Tb 158.93 / 65	Dy 162.51 / 66	Ho 164.94 / 67	Er 167.27 / 68	Tm 168.94 / 69	Yb 173.4 / 70
Actinide Series	Ac 227 / 89	Th 232.05 / 90	Pa 231 / 91	U 238.07 / 92	Np 237 / 93	Pu 242 / 94	Am 243 / 95	Cm 245 / 96	Bk 249 / 97	Cf 249 / 98	Es 255 / 99	Fm 255 / 100	Md 256 / 101	No 253 / 102

Software Application

Microsoft Excel

Using the Template

1. The Periodic Table template provides a reference for the Periodic Table of Elements. Students can either open the template in *Excel* whenever they need to refer to the Periodic Table or print it to keep as a reference.

2. Before printing the worksheet, you may want to make sure that the page is set to print Landscape (or horizontal) so that the entire table prints out on one page. Go to the **File** menu and select **Page Setup**.

Periodic Table *(cont.)*

3. Click the **Page** tab. Make sure that the box or circle beside **Landscape** is selected. Select **Print** if you want to print the document or **OK** to return to the worksheet.

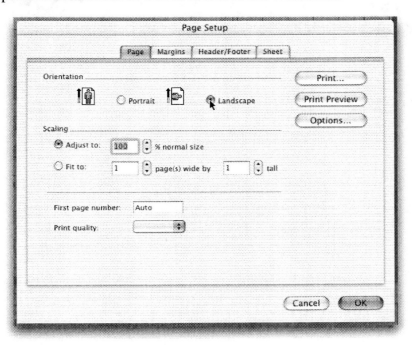

Tips and Tricks

- When you open the worksheet, you may get a warning about Macros in the document. Select **Enable Macros**. If you disable the macros, the worksheet will not work correctly.

Extension Idea

- Have students create posters about the elements. Assign elements to them and have them use the Periodic Table template first to learn the name, number, and atomic weight of their elements. They can use the Internet to research more information about their elements and then use *Microsoft PowerPoint* or *Microsoft Word* to create their posters.

Polls and Surveys

Importance Scale Survey

School Survey

Name: _____
Age: _____
Gender: _____

1	Not important at all
2	Somewhat unimportant
3	No opinion either way
4	Somewhat Important
5	Extremely Important

For each question below, circle the number to the right that on the importance of the issue. Use the scale above to mat

Question
1. Add your own question
2. Add your own question
3. Add your own question
4. Add your own question
5. Add your own question
6. Add your own question
7. Add your own question
8. Add your own question
9. Add your own question
10. Add your own question
11. Add your own question
12. Add your own question

Quality Comparison Survey

School Survey

Name: _____
Age: _____
Gender: _____

1	Poor
2	Fair
3	Good
4	Very Good

Quality Scale Survey

School Survey

Name: _____
Age: _____
Gender: _____

1	Poor
2	Fair
3	Good
4	Very Good
5	Excellent

For each Item identified below, circle the number to the right that best fits your judgement of its quality. Use the scale above to select the Quality number.

Description / Identification of Survey Item	Scale
1. Insert an Item Description or leave blank	1 2 3 4 5
2. Insert an Item Description or leave blank	1 2 3 4 5
3. Insert an Item Description or leave blank	1 2 3 4 5
4. Insert an Item Description or leave blank	1 2 3 4 5
5. Insert an Item Description or leave blank	1 2 3 4 5
6. Insert an Item Description or leave blank	1 2 3 4 5
7. Insert an Item Description or leave blank	1 2 3 4 5
8. Insert an Item Description or leave blank	1 2 3 4 5
9. Insert an Item Description or leave blank	1 2 3 4 5
10. Insert an Item Description or leave blank	1 2 3 4 5
11. Insert an Item Description or leave blank	1 2 3 4 5
12. Insert an Item Description or leave blank	1 2 3 4 5

ght that best fits your t the Quality number.

	Scale
ription	1 2 3 4 5
ription	1 2 3 4 5
ription	1 2 3 4 5
ription	1 2 3 4 5
ription	1 2 3 4 5
ription	1 2 3 4 5
ription	1 2 3 4 5
ription	1 2 3 4 5
ription	1 2 3 4 5
ription	1 2 3 4 5
ription	1 2 3 4 5
ription	1 2 3 4 5

Software Application

Microsoft Word

Using the Template

1. The Polls and Surveys template consists of three surveys—Importance Scale, Quality Comparison, and Quality Scale. Each survey is its own separate page in the document. Have students scroll down until they find the survey they wish to use.

2. Allow students to make any changes to the information at the top of the page, such as replacing text or deleting a line.

3. To add their own information to the template, students can click in the section that reads **Add Your Own Question, Item Description**, or **Insert an Item Description or leave blank**. They can type their own information to replace it.

4. Allow students to print the survey and make as many copies as necessary before distributing the survey. Have each person surveyed use the scale to determine his or her answer.

Polls and Surveys *(cont.)*

Tips and Tricks

- When you open the worksheet, you may get a warning about Macros in the document. Select **Enable Macros**. If you disable the macros, the worksheet will not work correctly.
- Students can replace the text in the scale with text with their own words. Have them click in the scale table and select one of the criteria. Then they can type their own text.

  If they need to make the table longer in able to fit the text they have added, students can move the mouse to the border at the end of the last column until the pointer becomes a double-headed arrow. Then they can click and drag to increase the width of the column.

1	I don't like it at
2	I don't love it.
3	It's OK.
4	I like it.
5	My Favorite!

1	I don't like it at all!
2	I don't love it.
3	It's OK.
4	I like it.
5	My Favorite!

Extension Idea

- Students can use the Polls and Surveys template as part of a research project or a paper on a political issue. They can survey a variety of classmates as well as friends and family to get range of opinions.

Reading Log

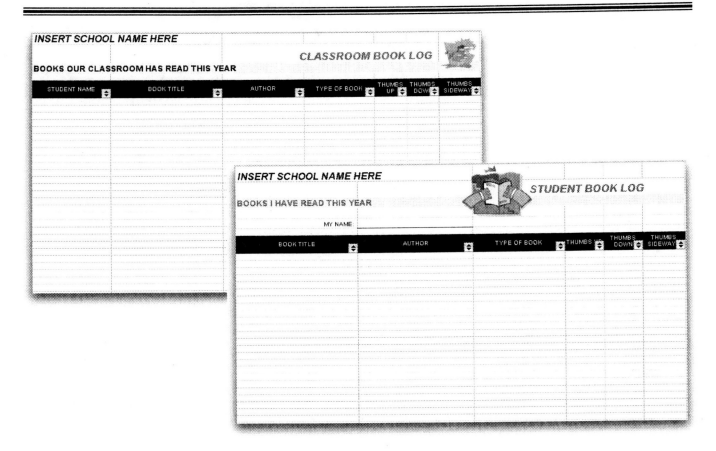

Software Application

Microsoft Excel

Modifying the Template

1. The Reading Log template has two worksheets—Classroom Book Log and Student Book Log. Have students click the tabs at the bottom of the workbook to access each one.

2. Directions for using the worksheets appear in text boxes. Students will need to delete these text boxes before typing their information into their reading logs. Students can print the worksheets before deleting the text boxes, or save the instructions in a separate *Excel* or *Word* document in order to access them again.

   To save in a separate document, have students click the border of the Student Book Log text box to select it, then go to the **Edit** menu and select **Copy**. Then they can go to a new document, go to the **Edit** menu again, and select **Paste**. They can repeat these steps to save the Classroom Book Log text box.

Reading Log *(cont.)*

3. To delete a text box, students can select its border and press the **backspace** or **delete** key.

4. Have students refer to the directions as they enter information into the book log. If you would like to have them enter data in a form as suggested in the **Note** section of the template, have students click the mouse to select a cell in the worksheet. Then they can go to the **Data** menu and select **Form**.

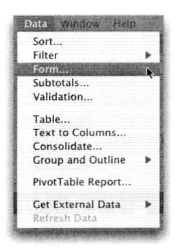

5. If students get a message that *Excel* does not know which cells contain column labels, have them click **OK** to tell *Excel* to use the first row of the selection as labels and not data. A form will appear for students to fill out with their book selections.

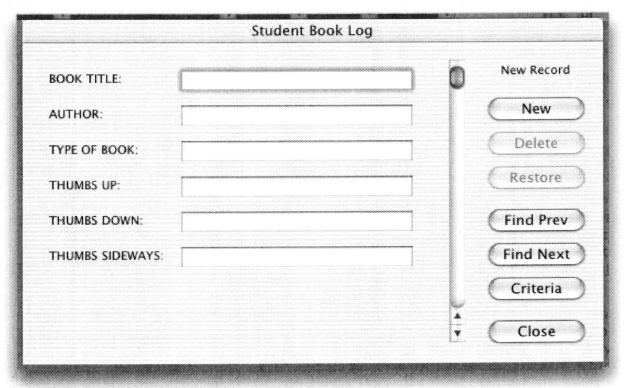

Reading Log *(cont.)*

6. Have students complete the form and select **New** after entering the information about each book. Show them how to use the **Tab** key to go from field to field. (If they use the enter or return key, the form will automatically move to the next entry.) When they have finished, they can click **Close** to close the form. The data has been entered into the worksheet.

MY NAME:	Annie Clougherty					
BOOK TITLE	**AUTHOR**	**TYPE OF BOOK**	**THUMBS UP**	**THUMBS DOWN**	**THUMBS SIDEWAYS**	
The Case of the Stolen Lunch Bag	Stuart Bateson	Fiction		X		
Harry Potter and the Goblet of Fire	J.K. Rowling	Fiction	X			
A Year in Antarctica	Frederick Kelly	Nonfiction		X		
The Thief Lord	Cornelia Funke	Fiction	X			
Hoot	Carl Hiaasen	Fiction	X			

Tips and Tricks

- The arrows included in each column indicate filters. Students can use filters to sort and hide data. For example, if they want to hide all the books which received a "Thumbs Down," they can use a filter to do so. Have them click the arrows to access the **Sort and Filter** menu.

  Students can select **Show Blanks** to show only the rows which have not received an "X" in the Thumbs Down column.

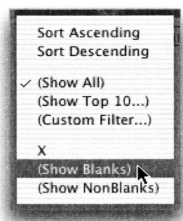

The worksheet will appear with all the "Thumbs Down" books hidden. The arrows appear in blue to indicate that a filter is being applied. To show all the books again, have students go to the **Sort and Filter** menu again and choose **Show All**.

MY NAME:	Annie Clougherty					
BOOK TITLE	**AUTHOR**	**TYPE OF BOOK**	**THUMBS UP**	**THUMBS DOWN**	**THUMBS SIDEWAYS**	
Harry Potter and the Goblet of Fire	J.K. Rowling	Fiction	X			
The Thief Lord	Cornelia Funke	Fiction	X			
Hoot	Carl Hiaasen	Fiction	X			

Recognition Certificates

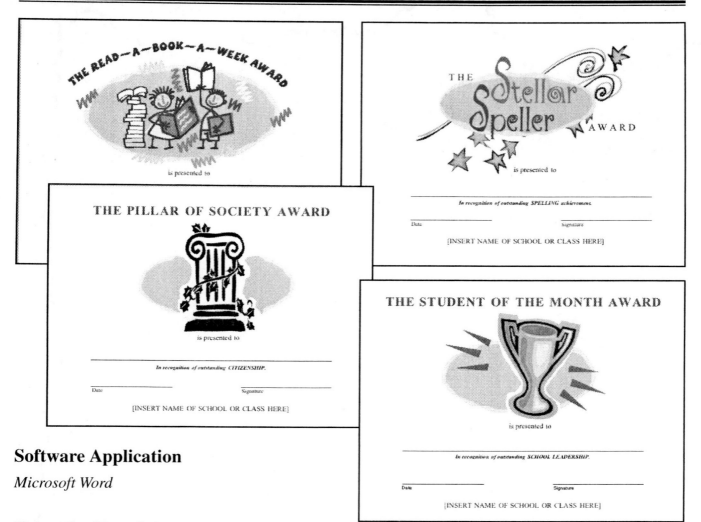

Software Application

Microsoft Word

Using the Template

1. Certificates provided in the Recognition Certificate template include the Read-a-Book-a-Week Award, Mighty Mathematician Award, Pillar of Society Award, The Sensational Scientist Award, The Stellar Speller Award, and the Student of the Month Award. Have students scroll down to find the template they wish to use.

2. Have students use the mouse to select the words **Insert Name of School or Class Here**. Make sure that they have selected the brackets along with the text. Then they can type the name of their school or class.

3. Have students click the mouse on the first line and type the name of the certificate recipient. To increase the font size or change the font style, students can use the mouse to select the name, then use the Formatting Toolbar or the **Format➜Font** menu to make their changes.

4. Have students click the **Date** line and type the date for the award.

5. To print the file, students can click the printer icon in the toolbar or select **File➜Print**. The template is formatted to print in *Landscape*, or horizontal, orientation. For best results, allow students to print this template on a color printer.

Recognition Certificates *(cont.)*

Tips and Tricks

- If students have trouble moving their graphic, have them select the graphic, click the **Format** menu, and select **Picture**. If they are using *Microsoft Word* 97 or 98, students should click the **Position** tab and select **Float Over Text**. (This step is not necessary for later versions of *Word*.) Then they can select how they would like the text to wrap around the picture.

Extension Idea

- Students can modify the text on the Pillar of Society Award, the Sensational Scientist Award, or the Student of the Month Award, if desired. They can create certificates for friends or classmates in honor of special occasions.

  To replace a graphic, students can use the mouse to select the existing graphic and press backspace or delete on the keyboard. Then they can go to the **Insert** menu and select **Picture**.

  If you would like students to use a graphic from the clip art gallery that comes with *Microsoft Office*, have them select **Clip Art**. The Clip Art Gallery will open. Students can look through the categories until they find a graphic that is appropriate for the award. They can select the graphic and click **Insert** to add it to the document. Have them close the Clip Art Gallery to return to *Microsoft Word*.

  If you have graphics in your files that you would like to students to use, have them select **From File**. They can locate the graphic they wish to use and click **Insert** to add it to the document.

  Once they have added the graphic, students can select it with the mouse and drag it into the area of the award in which they want it to appear. They can then use the mouse to resize it by clicking on a grabber handle and dragging the mouse until the graphic is the size that they want.

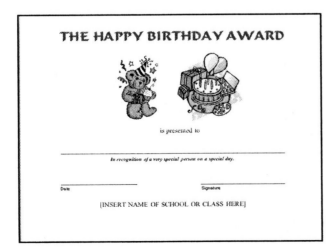

Schedules

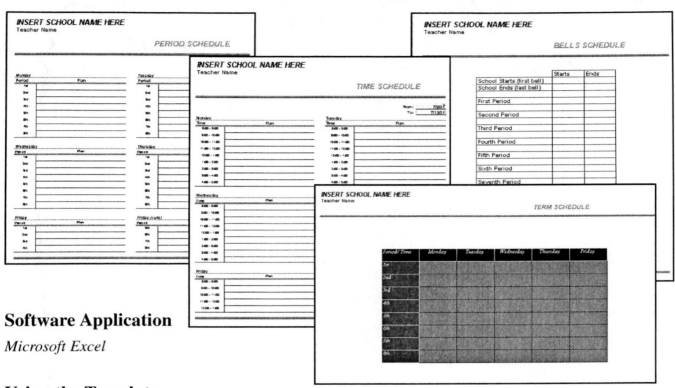

Software Application

Microsoft Excel

Using the Template

1. The Schedules template has four separate worksheets with different schedule options—By Period, By Time, Bells, and Term. Students can select a worksheet by clicking on its tab at the bottom of the workbook.

2. Have students select the **Insert School Name Here** text and replace it with the name of their school. Then they can select the **Teacher Name** text and replace it with the teacher's name.

3. If students are using the By Period Schedule or the By Time Schedule, have them type the starting date in the **From:** line. The red arrow that appears in this cell indicates that a comment is attached. Show students how to view the comment by moving the mouse over the cell. In this case, the comment tells students that if they enter the date of the Monday of the week, *Excel* will automatically add the date of the Friday of the week.

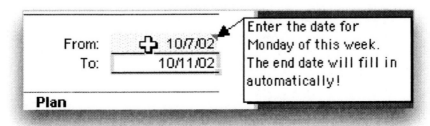

Schedules *(cont.)*

4. Have students type their schedules into the spaces provided.

Tips and Tricks

- When students open the worksheet, they may get a warning about Macros in the document. Have them select **Enable Macros**. If they disable the macros, the worksheet will not work correctly.

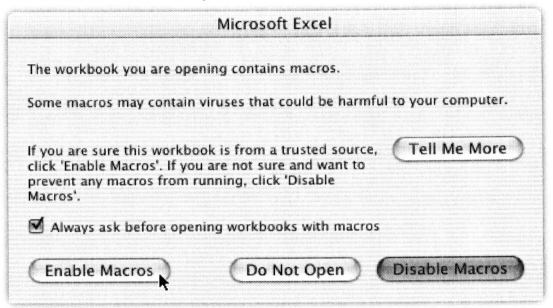

- Students can modify the Term Schedule worksheet to use as a means of keeping track of assignments. Have them replace the **Period/Time** text with the word **Assignments**. They can also replace the **1st**, **2nd**, **3rd**, and so on text with the names of the subjects they are taking. Then they can print the worksheet, make copies, and write down their assignments each week.

Assignments	Monday	Tuesday	Wednesday	Thursday	Friday
Math					
Social Studies					
Language Arts					
Science					
Elective					

School Reports

REPORT TITLE

By

[Your Name]

[Your Instructor's Name]

[Your Class]

[The Date]

OUTLINE TITLE

Introduction:

I. The first sub-topic

    A. First supporting information for the sub-topic

        1. Detail of the information

        2. Detail of the information

    B. Second supporting information for the sub-topic

        1. Detail of the information

        2. Detail of the information

II. The second sub-topic

    A. First supporting information for the sub-topic

        1. Detail of the information

Software Application

Microsoft Word

Using the Template

1. When students open this template, they have the option of creating a Formal, Simple, Standard, Book, Essay, or Term Paper report.

2. The title page of the template in the *Word* document is an example of a typical title page or cover page that would be used for a report. It can either be provided to students as an example or a student could highlight each line on the page, delete the content of the line and then type in the specific content for the line as it relates to the student's report.

3. The outline page provides an explanation of an outline showing its proper format and suggesting the content of each section of the outline. Again, this page could be provided to students as a reference to help them make their outlines, or students could highlight each line on the page, delete the content suggestion for the line, and then type in the specific content for the line as it relates to the project.

4. The first page of the Written Report instructs students to put all necessary personal information at the top-left of their page. Students are reminded to indent and double-space all paragraphs in the body of the report.

5. The Works Cited page provides only basic information about citing the material used in the report. Adding to this page by providing samples of different reference types would be helpful to students. Students could use the examples to guide them as they added their own references. They could delete the examples when they were finished.

School Reports *(cont.)*

6. The Checklist template provides an excellent checklist for students to use while they are working on the outline, the paper itself and the references cited. This checklist can be used as is or modified by the teacher or student. To delete text, simply highlight the words to be deleted, one section at a time, and then press the **Delete** or **Backspace** key. To add text, move the cursor to the space where the text is to be added and then type in the text that is to be added. **Note:** Only one section can be worked on at a time. If the text to be removed or added is in several places, students will need to click on each section.

7. Tips for Writing Your Report provides tips in three sections: Create a Schedule, Add Interest, and Make Every Word Count. Again, these can be provided for student use as is, or teachers or students can modify the list, as suggested in the checklist.

Extension Ideas:

- **Model Report Writing**: Have students work with different sections of a report that were already written. They can work in groups and have the members of the group help by suggesting ways to change and improve the report. As the work progresses and ideas are developed, have the students track their suggestions, showing different drafts of the work and the changes that were suggested and then completed. Make the experience a collaborative one in which students feel comfortable making suggestions and making changes.

- **Group Generated "Checklist for Writing"**: The checklist provided with the template is a good one, but as with anything, improvement is possible. Have students brainstorm additional ideas that, if added to the checklist, would provide more assistance to them when writing the report. The same categories—The Outline, The Paper, Works Cited—could remain and additional topics could be added, too. Students offer their own unique writing history, as well as their own areas of awareness and perspective, and are often able to provide checking details left out by teachers.

- **Group Generated "Tips for Writing Your Report"**: As with generating additional items for the checklist, students are often able to add ideas here, too. What one student has done to make his/her report a success is often not shared with others, though sharing these experiences is valuable. Not every student thinks or processes the same way or learns from the same successes or failures. When the comfort level allows students to share their ideas easily without fear, students can share their writing experiences—what has turned out well or not turned out well.

Science Fair Project

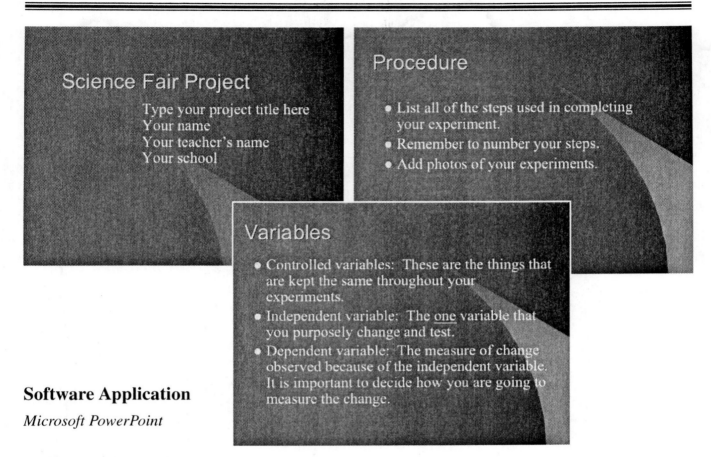

Software Application

Microsoft PowerPoint

Using the Template

1. The Science Fair Project template consists of eleven slides—Title, Statement of the Problem, Project Overview, Research, Variables, Hypothesis, Materials, Procedure, Data/Observations, Conclusion, and Works Cited. You can scroll down to view all the slides in the project.

2. Have students go to the Title slide and select the **Type your project title here** text. Have them type their project's title. Have them do the same to add their names, teacher's name, and school.

3. Have students scroll to the second slide. They can select the text and replace it by typing the problem that they will be investigating.

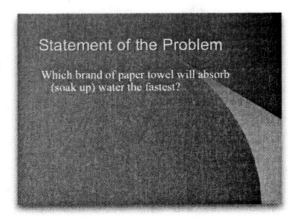

Science Fair Project *(cont.)*

4. Have students scroll to the third slide. They can select the text and replace it with a brief summary or overview of their project.

5. Have students scroll to the fourth slide. Have them replace the text that appears after the bullets with information about their research. If they do not need all five bullets, they can delete the additional bullets from the slide. After they have finished, they can delete the **Summarize your research here in three to five main bullet points:** text.

6. Have students scroll to the fifth slide. Have them select the text after **Controlled Variables:** and enter the information about the controlled variables for their experiment. Have them do the same for **Independent Variable:** and **Dependent Variable:**.

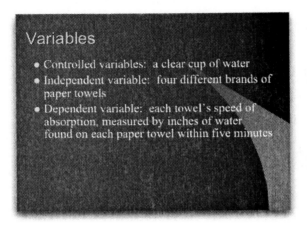

7. Have students scroll to the sixth slide. Have them select the text under **Hypothesis** and replace it with their hypotheses for the experiment.

8. Have students scroll to the seventh slide. Have them replace the bulleted text with information about the materials that they used. If they need to add more bullets to the list, have them simply press **enter** or **return** after the last line. This will add a new bullet and bring the cursor to the next line.

9. Have students scroll to the eighth slide. Have them enter the information about the steps of their procedure. If they need one or more additional slides for this information, have them go to the **Insert** menu and select **Duplicate Slide**.

Science Fair Project *(cont.)*

This will add another **Procedure** slide to the presentation. If you are in Outline view (or Normal view for *Microsoft PowerPoint 2000/2001* or *XP/X*) or Slide Sorter view, you can see that the duplicate slide has been added as the new slide number 9. Students can then continue adding information about the procedure of their experiments, adding additional slides when necessary.

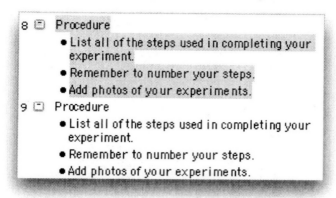

10. Have students scroll to the **Data/Observations** slide and describe the results of their experiments. They can add a chart created in *Microsoft Excel* or use the *Microsoft Graph* feature. Have them go to the **Insert** menu and select **Chart**. They might want to delete the text on the slide before creating the chart.

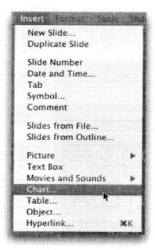

The *Microsoft Graph* feature will open. If students do not have a chart from *Excel* to add, have them use *Microsoft Graph* to create one. If they do have a chart to add, have them select the datasheet window (which looks like a worksheet), not the graph. Then have them go to the **File** menu and select **Import File**. Then they can navigate to the *Excel* file and add it to the slide.

Science Fair Project *(cont.)*

11. Have students scroll to the Conclusions slide. Have them select the text and type a brief summary of their findings.

12. Have students scroll to the Works Cited slide. Have them select the text and add their sources—both print and electronic.

Tips and Tricks

- If necessary, you can increase the size of a text box on a slide. Click the text to make the text box visible. Then click one of the corners of the text box and drag until there is enough room for your text.

- If you want to add a graphic to a slide, go to the **Insert** menu and select **Picture**. If you want to add clip art, select **From Clip Art**. If you want to add a graphic from your file, select **From File**. Navigate to the graphic and add it to your document.

Extension Ideas

Have students try some of the following science project ideas and use the template to create their reports.

- Do living plants give off moisture?
- Do plants grow better in sand or clay?
- Does sound travel better through solids, liquids, or gasses?
- How far does a worm travel in five minutes?
- How long does bread mold take to grow?
- Can most people tell the difference between a name brand and a generic soda of the same type?
- On what part of the tongue do most people taste a sweet taste?
- How much salt must be added to a glass of water for an egg to float?
- At room temperature, does an ice cube melt faster in air or in water?

Story Map Outline

Insert Name of School Here

STORY MAP OUTLINE

Student Name:	
Story/Book Title:	
Author:	

THE SETTING

Characters: (Who are the main characters?)	
Place: (Where does the story take place?)	
Time: (When does the story take place?)	

PROBLEM/GOAL: (What started the chain of

List in order the major events that lead to the goal or resolution.	Event 1:	
	Event 2:	
	Event 3:	
	Event 4:	
	Event 5:	
	Event 6:	

THE RESOLUTION: (What finally happens? Is the goal reached and the problem solved? Explain.)

Software Application

Microsoft Word

Using the Template

1. This template provides a format or framework for organizing the content of a story or book. It is designed to have students enter the information required into different sections of the outline: The Setting, The Problem, The Events, and The Resolution.

2. To insert the name of the school or class, the **Insert Name of School Here** text must be highlighted and then deleted. Then the school or class name can be typed into the space created.

3. To enter their names, story or book titles, and author information, students can click in the box to the right of the information title and type in the required information. If more space is needed, another line will be added to the box.

Tips and Tricks

- The three sections of the template that have cells are actually tables that have been placed in the *Word* document. The cells of the tables can be altered. Cell size can be changed, or cells can be added or deleted all together.

Story Map Outline *(cont.)*

- **Changing Cell Size and Content**: To make a cell wider or narrower by moving its border, move the cursor on the line to be moved until it displays a small left and right arrow on either side. Hold down the mouse button and drag the border to the desired position on the left or the right. To make a cell taller or shorter, do the same thing. The arrows on the cursor will be up and down and the line will move up or down when dragged. To take text out of a cell, highlight the words and press **Backspace** or **Delete**.

The Original Table

THE SETTING	
Characters: (Who are the main characters?)	
Place: (Where does the story take place?)	
Time: (When does the story take place?)	

The Changed Table

THE SETTING	
Characters:	
Place:	
Time:	

- **Deleting Text Boxes and Adding Text**: Highlight a text box that needs to be removed and select **Backspace** or **Delete**. Be sure to adjust the sizes of the neighboring cells or boxes so space is not left empty.

The Explanation Box that is located on the right needs to be deleted. This will allow more space to describe the event details.

List in order the major events that lead to the goal or resolution.	Event 1:	
	Event 2:	
	Event 3:	
	Event 4:	
	Event 5:	
	Event 6:	

This table's cells have been made larger to fill the space left by the deleted explanation box. More space is now available for the event descriptions that are to be added.

Event 1:	Pigs want to leave home, so they gather building materials.
Event 2:	The first pig makes his house out of straw.
Event 3:	The second pig makes his house out of sticks.
Event 4:	The third pig makes his house out of bricks.
Event 5:	The wolf tries to blow all the houses down and is successful, except for the third pig's brick house where all the pigs are hiding.
Event 6:	The wolf tries to come down the chimney of the third pig's house but he is caught and cooked for dinner.

Story Map Outline *(cont.)*

Pegasus School—Third Grade

STORY MAP REVIEW

Student Name:	Alex Figueroa
Story/Book Title:	The Three Little Pigs

THE SETTING

Characters:	The Three Little Pigs, a Mother Pig, and a Wolf
Place:	A little town in the English countryside
Time:	Spring, when all the flowers are blooming

GOAL: The Three Little Pigs decided that they were old enough to move out on their own. Their mother told them that they would need to build a big, strong house so that they would not be bothered by the Big, Bad Wolf.

Event 1:	Pigs want to leave home, so they gather building materials.
Event 2:	The first pig makes his house out of straw.
Event 3:	The second pig makes his house out of sticks.
Event 4:	The third pig makes his house out of bricks.
Event 5:	The wolf tries to blow all the houses down and is successful, except for the third pig's brick house where all the pigs are hiding.
Event 6:	The wolf tries to come down the chimney of the third pig's house but he is caught and cooked for dinner.

THE RESOLUTION: The wolf was caught and cooked for dinner, so the three little pigs did not have to worry about him anymore.

The example above shows how a student, describing the story of "The Three Little Pigs," used this template. The framework for the template is standard—all the student has to do is click in each text box and add the relevant information. This template format helps students grasp the concept of summarizing a story or a book's content. The space provided for entering text is minimal to encourage students to be brief when they present the main idea of the story.

Extension Ideas

- **Historical Time Line:** This Story Map Outline concept can be used to map other subjects as well. Time lines of events in history also have similar characteristics to reporting on story content.

Story Map Outline *(cont.)*

Replace the headings in the Story Map Outline with the headings shown below and adjust the spaces accordingly.

Historical Time Line

Student Name
Event in History

Setting:
Date in History
Location in the World
Individuals Involved

Details of the Event
   1.   **4.**
   2.   **5.**
   3.   **6.**

Resolution and Consequences of the Event

- **Planning for a Class Party**: This template format can also provide the structure for organizing a class party. It helps focus the plan and makes it easier to save the details for the future.

Party Plans

Class Group:
Party Theme or Event Celebration:

Details:
Date and Time:
Location:
Individuals Helping

Details of the Event
   1.   **Game/Activity 1**   **4.   Game/Activity 4**
   2.   **Game/Activity 2**   **5.   Food and Refreshments**
   3.   **Game/Activity 3**   **6.   Party Favors**

Clean Up Details:
Suggestions for the Future

Taking Notes and Outlining

TAKING NOTES

1 **Name the source.** Include all the information you'll [...] the source in a bibliography: name of the publication, chapter o[...] publisher, and date of publication.

2 **Write a summary.** What are the main ideas or opi[...] If possible, use key words and phrases from the source in your [...] sentence.

3 **List the important details.** Identify specific det[...] support the main ideas. When you include the exact words of th[...] another speaker, use quotation marks to identify the beginning [...] text.

CHECKLIST FOR WRITING AN OUTLINE

1 **Organization**

- ☐ The introduction states the main topic or idea of the outline.
- ☐ Each paragraph in your paper has a sub-topic.
- ☐ Each sub-topic describes the main idea for a paragraph.
- ☐ Supporting information and details for a sub-topic are listed under the sub-topic.
- ☐ Each piece of supporting information is listed separately.
- ☐ When supporting information is listed under a sub-topic, there are at least two pieces of information in the list. If there is only one piece of information to support a sub-topic, the information is included in the sub-topic.
- ☐ The conclusion summarizes the main idea of the outline.

2 **Format**

- ☐ For a sentence outline:
  Each outline entry is a complete sentence with a period at the end of the sentence.
- ☐ For a topic outline:
  Each outline entry is a phrase with no punctuation at the end of the phrase.

3 **Spelling**

- ☐ All words are spelled correctly.
- ☐ All typing errors are corrected.

Software Application

Microsoft Word

Using the Template

1. This template has four sections: Outline Format Sheet, Checklist for Writing an Outline, Taking Notes Worksheet, and Developing a Paragraph Worksheet. Have students scroll to view the available worksheets.

2. The Taking Notes and Developing a Paragraph pages are designed to have students type their work directly onto the template without modifying the template. The boxes that are displayed are text boxes and are to be typed into directly. As the box fills and more space is needed, the box will automatically add a line until the student has finished.

3. The Checklist for Writing is a checklist for students to use as they create an outline. It is a *Word* document, so additional ideas can be included. Ideas can be changed and deleted. Sub-topics are accented with bullets. If a sub-topic one is added, the bullet will appear; or if one is deleted, the bullet will be removed. As with other template examples, students can brainstorm and modify this checklist to suit their individual needs.

Taking Notes and Outlining *(cont.)*

4. The Outline Format Sheet is an outline with each line defined for content. This *Word* document can be used the way it is, or students can replace each line with content that relates to their outlining.

Extension Ideas

- **Model Notes Bulletin Board**: Have students take notes to perfect their product. Post the notes on a bulleting board, highlighting aspects of exemplary notes. Students learn from others. Have students ask each other "How do your notes help you study?" and "What works best for you?" Make a summary of the comments to add to the bulletin board. Have students decorate the bulletin board with colorful graphics and note-taking slogans.

- **Miniature Reminders**: Have students make small, card-shaped "Taking Notes" and "Outlines" reminders that they can put in their notebooks or tape on their desks.

Outlines

Organizing Material

1. Introduction
2. 4–6 Subtopics with Supporting Information
3. Conclusion

Taking Notes

1. Name Sources
2. Write Summary
3. List the Important Details

Timeline

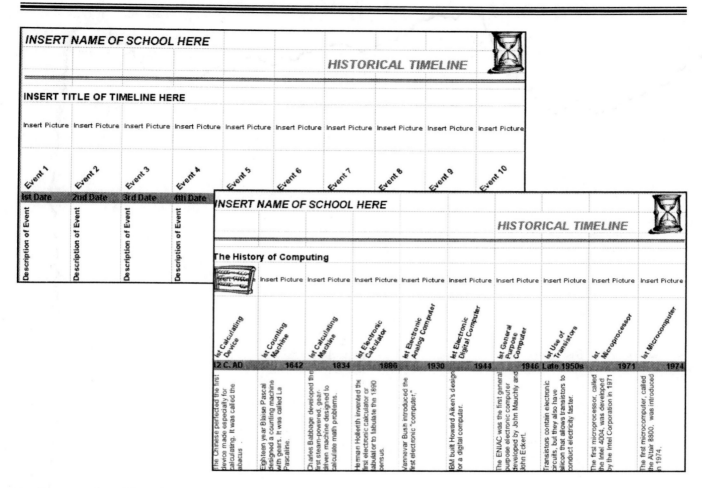

Software Application

Microsoft Excel

Using the Template

1. The Timeline template has two worksheets—one with the template itself and one with a sample timeline. (Sheet 3 is a blank worksheet.) Direct students to click the tabs to access the different worksheets.

2. Have students select the **Insert School Name Here** text and type the name of their school.

3. Students can select the **Insert Title of Timeline** text and replace it with a title for the timeline.

4. Have students click the **Event 1** cell and type the first event.

5. Have students type the date of the event in the **1st Date** cell.

Timeline *(cont.)*

6. Have students click in the first **Description of Event** cell. This cell has been formatted with the text at a 90-degree orientation. When students click in the cell and begin to type, the text will appear as it normally does. When they press **Enter** or **Return** or click in another cell, the text will appear at a 90-degree orientation again.

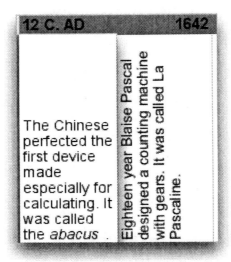

7. To add graphics of the events to the timeline, have students select the cell in which they are going to add the graphic. Have them go to the **Insert** menu and select **Picture**, then select **Clip Art** to add a graphic from the Microsoft Clip Gallery or **From File** to select a graphic from students' files.

8. Have students repeat steps 5, 6, and 7 for the remaining events in the timeline.

Tips and Tricks

- If students do not have graphics to add for each event, they can delete the **Insert Picture** text from the cells in row 5. Also, if there are fewer than 10 events in the timeline, students can delete the unneeded section of the timeline. Have them select the cells they want to delete text and formatting from, and go to **Edit** on the menu bar. Have them select **Clear** and then **All**.

- If students have more than 10 events, they can add on to the timeline. Have them use the mouse to select cells J5 through J8. Then they can go to the **Edit** menu and select **Copy**. Have them click in cell K5, go to the **Edit** menu, and select **Paste**. This will paste the cells complete with formatting. Students can paste again in as many cells as necessary. They may need to adjust the width of the columns to fit the text. Then they can replace the text with Event 11, Event 12, and so on until their timeline is complete.

Extension Ideas

- Have students create timelines for events for book reports, focusing on important plot and character developments.

- Have students create timelines for school projects, indicating deadlines and due dates.

To Do List

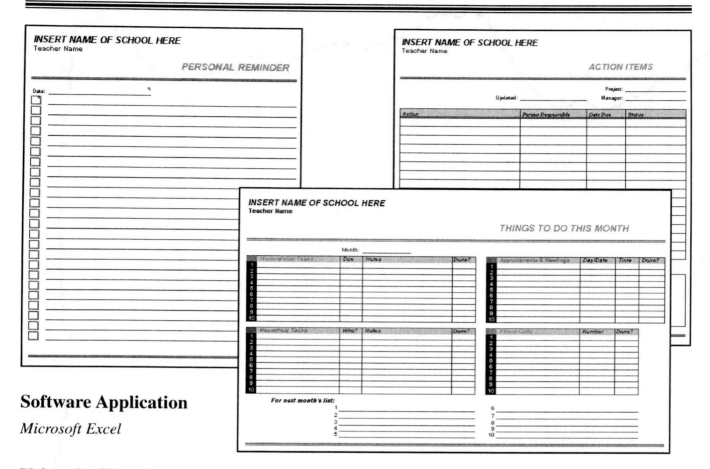

Software Application

Microsoft Excel

Using the Template

1. The To Do List template has three options—Personal Reminder, Action Items, and Things to Do This Month. Have students click a tab to select a worksheet.

2. Have students select the **Insert School Name Here** text and replace it with the name of their school.

3. The **Personal Reminder** worksheet has comments attached. The red arrows in the cells indicate that there is a comment. Show students how to view the comment by moving the mouse over the cell.

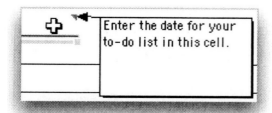

To Do List *(cont.)*

4. Students can either type the information in *Excel* or print and write by hand.

Extension Idea

- Students could use the Action Items template to keep track of assignments in a team project. Have them replace the **Action Items** text with the name or subject of the assignment. If it isn't needed, they can delete the **Project**, **Updated**, and **Manager** text.

  The team leader could type the task, the name of each team member responsible, and the date due on each line. Then they could print the worksheet and check off when each team member has completed his or her task.

Claremont Middle School
Mrs. Rojas

Reptiles Research Project

Action	Person Responsible	Date Due	Status
Research snakes	Amy	11/15/02	Done
Research lizards	Neil	11/15/02	Done
Research turtles	Kevin	11/15/02	
Outline	Kevin	11/22/02	
Write Introduction	Neil	11/22/02	

Word Scramble

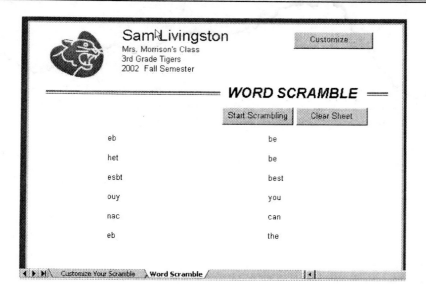

Software Application

Microsoft Excel

Using the Template

1. The Word Scramble template is a *Microsoft Excel* program that allows you to create a custom word scramble. To customize the header on the page, select **Customize** located in the top right hand corner of the template. Type your school and class information and include a logo. If you choose **Lock and Save Template,** this information will be saved permanently to your template. If you choose **Lock but Don't Save**, the information will be kept for the duration of your Word Scramble creation, but the changes will not be saved to the template.

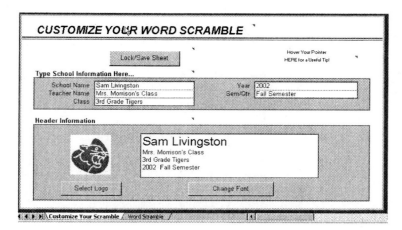

2. A word list will need to be added to the template. To enter the words, select **Word Scramble** at the bottom of the template. Then select **Start Scrambling**. Enter the number of words that will be used in the puzzle and, when directed, enter each word, one at a time. Once the words have been entered, a puzzle page will be created and the words will be scrambled.

Word Scramble *(cont.)*

3. Notice in the finished example that the letters of each of the individual words have been scrambled and that the order of the words for the sentences has been changed, too.

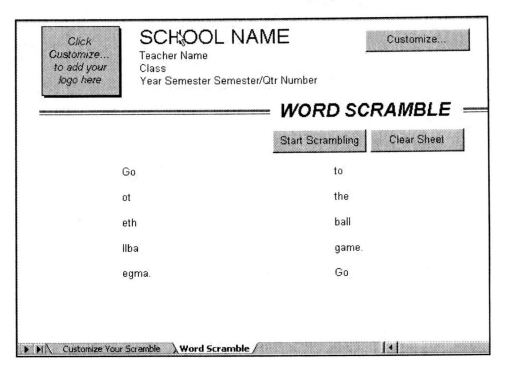

Extension Ideas

- **Class Problem Solving Game Activity:** Have students create a Word Scramble and then have them trade with other students to solve each other's scramble. Use themes with limits set for the content of the word scramble:

    Riddles with Scrambled Solutions

    Famous Quotations

    Motivational Sayings

    Grammatical Rules

    Historical Events

    Science Equations

- **Provide Clues:** Have students provide clues to help with the solution as time taken for solving the scramble goes by... a 1 Minute Clue, 2 Minute Clue, 5 Minute Clue and so on.
- **Award Points:** Award points for the solution based on time taken to solve the scramble. For example, 5 points for less than 1 minute, 4 points for less than 2 minutes, and so on.
- **Educational Value:** Remember the educational value of this task lies in its strength to help students remember important information and concepts and to provide students with fun problem solving activities that will strengthen their problem solving abilities.

Workplace Skills

Software Application

Microsoft Word

Using the Template

1. The Workplace Skills template is a two-page job application. Have students scroll down to view both pages of the template.

2. Have students select the **Insert School Name Here** text and replace it with the name of their school.

3. Students can click in each field to add the required information. For options like Full Time or Part Time, or yes or no questions, have them type an "X" in the appropriate box.

Workplace Skills *(cont.)*

4. Instruct students to leave blank any fields which do not apply to them, such as **Driver's License Number** if they are too young to have a driver's license.

5. When students complete the application, have them print it, and then sign and date it on the second page.

Extension Ideas

- Have students complete the job applications as part of a simulation activity.
- The template can be adapted for students to use to apply for a position at school, such as reporter for the school newspaper.

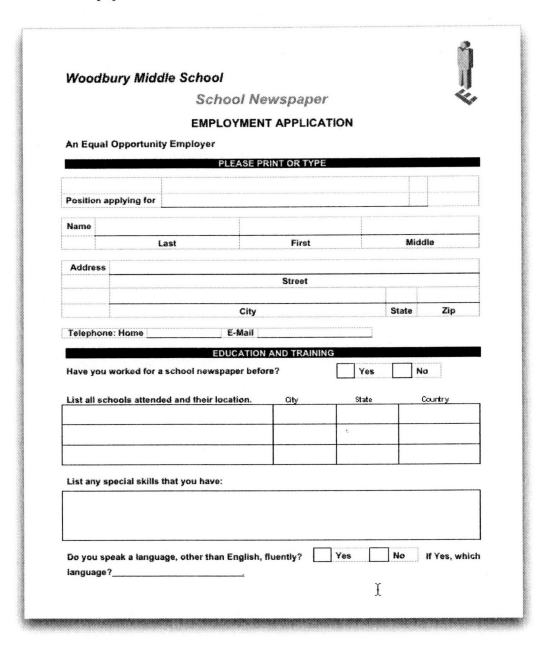

Writing Checklist

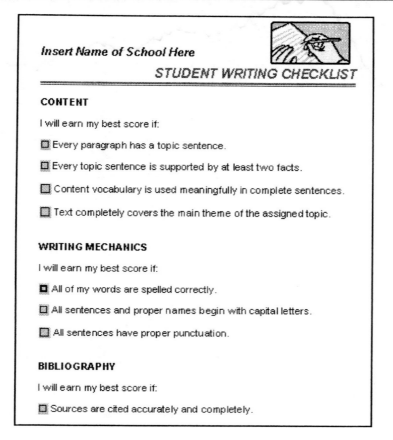

Software Application

Microsoft Word

Using the Template

1. This *Word* document lists different criteria that will help a student create a successful writing project. The template can be printed as-is by going to the **File** menu and selecting **Print**. This summary sheet could then be used for reference.

2. If this template sheet is used on the computer, each check box when selected will need to have an "x" added when the criteria has been met. This is a way for students to record what they have checked as they edit their writing. The template is locked and protected so that it cannot be changed. Only an "x" in a check box can be added or taken away.

CONTENT

I will earn my best score if:

☒ Every paragraph has a topic sentence.

☒ Every topic sentence is supported by at least two facts.

Writing Checklist *(cont.)*

3. The template must be unlocked in order to make changes to it. Select the **Tools** menu, then click **Unprotect Document**. Changes can now be made to the document. To protect the document when you are finished making changes, go to the **Tools** menu again and select **Protect Document**.

Tips and Tricks

• When you are designing or changing a template or form, it is a good idea to have your Forms toolbar showing. You can quickly protect the form or remove its protection by selecting the **Protect Form** button on the Forms toolbar.

Extension Idea

• **Changing a Form:** Use this basic form to teach student how to change forms. Have the students make a variety of changes to this form to help them understand the techniques that are used in form making. To begin, have students work with:

Changing the Status of a Form from Protected to Unprotected

Changing and Inserting Text

Adding a Check Box

Shading a Form Field

Have the students display their various changes to this form and share how they made the changes.

• **Making a New Form:** Following up on the skills learned when students were changing the Writing Checklist Form, have the students make new forms to help them with reviewing and editing their work. Topics to include:

Spell Check Reminders

Basic Grammar Rules Worth Remembering

Punctuation Reminders

Proper Format for Citing Paper Resources

Proper Format for Citing Online Resources

Allow the students to gather ideas and make different forms. Then have students pool their ideas and discuss the similarities and differences with their presentation and their focus. Following this, encourage the students to review all the ideas, then create their own checklists to suit their own needs and learning style.

Writing Rubric

Insert Name of School Here

NOTE: The specific criteria for each category are meant to serve only as a guide. You may want to insert your own criteria based on your own standards. *Delete this text box before printing.*

WRITING RUBRIC

CATEGORY	4	3	2	1
Topic Sentence	Each paragraph starts with a well-constructed and focused topic sentence.	Almost all paragraphs start with a well-constructed topic sentence.	The topic sentences are not well constructed and they don't focus on one topic.	Paragraphs do not start with a sentence with a focused topic.
Supporting Details	Each paragraph contains 2 or 3 details that support the topic.	Each paragraph contains at least 2 details that support the topic.	Each paragraph contains at least 1 detail that supports the topic.	Paragraphs do not contain details that support the topic.
Vocabulary	Vivid words and phrases are used that bring the topic alive and are used accurately.	Vivid words and phrases are used that bring the topic alive and they may not always be used accurately.	The vocabulary words used clearly communicate ideas but there is a lack of variety.	The vocabulary used is limited and does not adequately communicate ideas.
Grammar & Spelling	There are no errors in grammar or spelling.	There are 1 or 2 errors in grammar or spelling but they don't affect meaning.	There are 3 or 4 errors in grammar or spelling that distract the reader from the content.	There are more than 4 errors in grammar or spelling that make the paper difficult to understand.
Capitalization & Punctuation	There are no errors in capitalization or punctuation.	There are 1 or 2 errors in capitalization and/or punctuation but the paper is still easy to understand.	There are a few errors in capitalization and/or punctuation that distracts from the content.	There are more than four errors in capitalization and/or punctuation that make the paper difficult to understand.
Conclusion	The conclusion is well constructed and draws together all the details to form an ending.	There is a conclusion and it draws together most of the details.	There is a conclusion but it doesn't draw together most of the details.	There is no clear conclusion or ending to the paper.

Software Application

Microsoft Word

Using the Template

1. This template is a rubric that can be used to help with grading a writing project. It is a table with text in each of its cells. To personalize the rubric, go to the section at the top left of the template. Delete the **Insert Name of School Here** text that is there and add your school name or your name and class. Also, remove the section with the instructions.

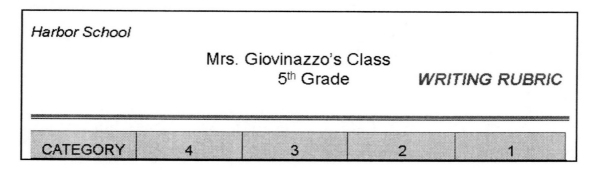

2. To print the rubric, go to the **File** menu and select **Print**.

Writing Rubric *(cont.)*

3. The text in the template can be modified in many ways. To change the content of the text, highlight the text that needs to be changed and type in the replacement text.

> Vivid words and phrases are used that bring the topic alive and they may not always be used accurately.

> Vivid words and phrases are used that bring the topic alive **although they are not** always used **correctly**.

4. Font selection, size, color, boldness, and alignment can all be altered, too. Select the text to be changed by highlighting it. Then select the font format that needs changing. Continue with other changes while the text area is highlighted.

CATEGORY	4
Topic Sentence	Each paragraph starts with a well-constructed and focused topic sentence.
Supporting Details	Each paragraph contains 2 or 3 details that support the topic.

CATEGORY	4
Topic Sentence	Each paragraph starts with a well-constructed and focused topic sentence.
Supporting Details	Each paragraph contains 2 or 3 details that support the topic.

5. Background color and cell color can also be changed. To change the background color of the entire page, select **Format** on the **Menu Bar**, go down to **Background**, and over to the color choices. Pick one of the Standard Colors or go to **More Colors** or **Fill Effects**. Play with these choices, as the results can be surprising!

Writing Rubric *(cont.)*

6. It is possible to add text to a cell to the point where more space is needed. When this happens, a line will automatically be added to the cell. Normally this doesn't cause a problem, but if you are adding a lot to different cells, your rubric may go over its one page format. To compensate, try selecting smaller fonts or making the font you do have smaller in size. You will need to change all the cells to make the format uniform. To change all the cells, highlight them and then change the font and/or its size. The example below shows how different fonts can be different in size even when the font size selected is the same. Helvetica font is larger than Times font and a size of 12 is larger than a size of 10.

Topic Sentence (Helvetica 12)　　　**Topic Sentence** (Helvetica 10)

Topic Sentence (Times 12)　　　**Topic Sentence** (Times 10)

Extension Ideas

- **Rubric Websites:** Many rubric websites are available to teachers. Teachers can use them to decide on grading criteria and to help students focus on editing their work effectively to produce top quality work. Use keywords or search words like **educational rubrics** or try **Kathy Schrock's Guide for Educators** Web Site at Discover School. The lists of assessment ideas and examples are endless and of high quality.

- **Brainstorming Project Parameters and Rubric Criteria**: It has long been acknowledged that students who invest time offering input into the construction of a project and its assessment will do a better job on the project. The following process involves students to a greater degree than is usually found in traditional classroom practices:

  1. Present a barebones project idea. Give the curriculum content focus.

  2. Have students brainstorm different ways they could learn and remember the material.

  3. Create several groups. Have each group summarize the different ideas presented.

  4. Have each group present an idea for learning and presenting the materials learned.

  5. Encourage the use of technology in the process.

  6. Have each group design a rubric that will assess:

     What learning took place?

     What concepts were remembered?

     What concepts could be applied in other situations?

Template Tips and Tricks

Templates that have been saved in the *Microsoft Office* application folder can be accessed in several different ways. With any version of *Office*, you can go to the **File** menu, select **Open**, and navigate to the **Templates** folder in your version of *Microsoft Office*. From there you can open the **Teacher Tools** or **Student Tools** folder, select a template, and click the **Open** button.

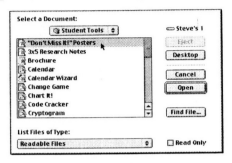

If you have *Microsoft Office 97, 98,* or *2000*, you can also access the templates by going to the **File** menu and selecting **New**. This will open the New Document menu. From here you can click on the **Teacher Tools** or **Student Tools** tab and then select the name of the template.

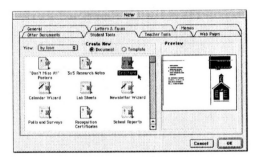

If you have *Microsoft Office XP*, the simplest method of accessing the templates is the Template Gallery. In *Microsoft Office 2001* or *X*, this is called the Project Gallery. Click on the **Teacher Tools** or **Student Tools** category and then select the template.

The template will open as a new document. For student projects, you may want to create individual folders in which students can save their files. Show them how to save their files by selecting **Save** from the **File** menu or clicking the **Save** icon on the standard toolbar.

Remind students to save their files often. Show them how to turn on the **AutoRecover** feature in the **Options** (Windows) or **Preferences** (Macintosh) menu. The *Microsoft Office* application will create an AutoRecover file every ten minutes (or whichever amount of time you select). This way, if the computer crashes or loses power, students may be able to save information that might otherwise be lost.

Template Tips and Tricks *(cont.)*

You can also create your own *Microsoft Office* templates for your students to use. To do this, create your document, then go to the **File** menu and select **Save As**.

The Save As dialog box will open. Select **Document Template** in the Format: menu. The Microsoft Office application will automatically add the ".dot" extension and open the Templates folder. Click **Save**.

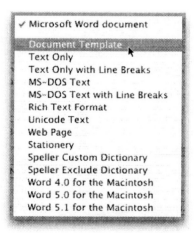

If you make changes to a Teacher Tools or Student Tools template, and you want to save these changes to the template itself, the simplest method might be to save over the existing template. For example, if you added your school name and teacher name to the Schedules template, you might want that information to appear every time you opened the template. You could do this by saving the file in the Student Tools folder as a document template with the exact same name. When you get a warning message that a file already exists with that name, click **OK** to replace the file.

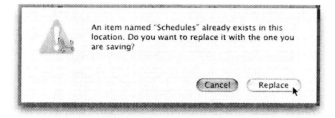

It's a good idea to keep the templates CD around in case you ever want to restore the original file.

Index of Activities and Software Applications

Teacher Templates

Template Name	Page Number in book	Microsoft Word	Microsoft Excel	Microsoft PowerPoint
"Don't Miss It!" Posters	6	X		
Brochure	8	X		
Calendar	10		X	
Calendar Wizard	12	X		
Class Welcome	15			X
Field Trip Permission	17	X		
Fractions Graphing	19		X	
Fundraising	21		X	
Gradebook	23		X	
Grant Request Letter (with Comments)	25	X		
Graph Paper	27		X	
Hall Pass (Restroom and Office)	29	X		
Inventory Control	30		X	
Lesson Plan	31	X		
Lists and Charts	33		X	
Medication Dispensing (Authorization)	34	X		
Music Paper	35		X	
Newsletter Wizard	36	X		
Overdue Book Notice	39	X		

Teacher Templates *(cont.)*

Template Name	Page Number in book	Microsoft Word	Microsoft Excel	Microsoft PowerPoint
"Don't Miss It!" Posters	6	X		
Brochure	8	X		
Calendar	10		X	
Calendar Wizard	12	X		
Class Welcome	15			X
Field Trip Permission	17	X		
Fractions Graphing	19		X	
Fundraising	21		X	
Gradebook	23		X	
Grant Request Letter (with Comments)	25	X		
Graph Paper	27		X	
Hall Pass (Restroom and Office)	29	X		
Inventory Control	30		X	
Lesson Plan	31	X		
Lists and Charts	33		X	
Medication Dispensing (Authorization)	34	X		
Music Paper	35		X	
Newsletter Wizard	36	X		
Overdue Book Notice	39	X		

Index of Activities and Software Applications (cont.)

Student Tools

Template Name	Page Numbers in Book	Curriculum Area	Microsoft Word	Microsoft Excel	Microsoft PowerPoint
3 x 5 Research Notes	72	Language Arts, Social Studies, Science, Mathematics	X		
Animal Quiz	76	Science			X
Brochure	79	Language Arts, Science, Social Studies, Mathematics	X		
Calendar	83	Social Studies		X	
Calendar Wizard	85	N/A	X	X	
Change Game	89	Mathematics		X	
Chart It!	93	Mathematics		X	
Country Report	98	Social Studies			X
Cryptogram	101	Language Arts		X	
"Don't Miss It!" Posters	104	Language Arts, Science, Social Studies	X		
Fractions Graphing	107	Mathematics		X	
Graph Paper	109	Mathematics		X	
Hangman	111	Language Arts		X	
Homework Recordkeeping	114	N/A		X	
Lab Sheets	116	Science	X		
Lists and Charts	119	N/A		X	
Make Your Own Minibook	121	Language Arts, Social Studies, Science, Mathematics			X

Index of Activities and Software Applications *(cont.)*

Student Tools

Template Name	Page Numbers in Book	Curriculum Area	Microsoft Word	Microsoft Excel	Microsoft PowerPoint
Newsletter Wizard	126	Language Arts, Social Studies	X		
Our Fifty States	130	Social Studies			X
Periodic Table	133	Science		X	
Polls and Surveys	135	Social Studies	X		
Reading Log	137	Language Arts		X	
Recognition Certificates	140	N/A	X		
Schedules	142	N/A		X	
School Reports	144	Language Arts, Social Studies, Science	X		
Science Fair Project	146	Science			X
Story Map Outline	150	Language Arts	X		
Taking Notes and Outlining	154	Language Arts, Social Studies, Science	X		
Timeline	156	Social Studies		X	
To Do List	158	N/A		X	
Word Scramble	160	Language Arts		X	
Workplace Skills	162	Social Studies	X		
Writing Checklist	164	Language Arts	X		
Writing Rubric	166	Language Arts	X		

CD-ROM Index

Teacher Tools Folder

"Don't Miss It!" Posters.dot

Brochure.dot

Calendar.xlt

Calendar Wizard.wiz

Class Welcome.pot

Field Trip Permission.dot

Fractions Graphing.xlt

Fundraising.xlt

Gradebook.xlt

Grant Request Letter .dot

Graph Paper.xlt

Hall Pass.dot

Lesson Plan.dot

Lists and Charts.xlt

Medication Dispensing.dot

Music Paper.xlt

Newsletter Wizard.wiz

Parent Bulletin.dot

Party Planner.xlt

Polls and Surveys.dot

Recognition Certificates.dot

Requisition Form.dot

Schedules.xlt

School Certificates.pot

Seating Chart.pot

Student Behavior Contract.dot

Student Database.xlt

Student Disciplinary Action.dot

Student Note.dot

Substitute Teacher Form.xlt

Syllabus.dot

Tests.dot

Thesis.dot

To Do List.xlt

Wise Reward.dot

Writing Rubric.dot

CD-ROM Index (cont.)

Student Tools Folder

3 x 5 Research Notes.dot

Animal Quiz.pot

Brochure.dot

Calendar.xlt

Calendar Wizard.wiz

Change Game.xlt

Chart It!.xlt

Country Report.pot

Cryptogram.xlt

"Don't Miss It!" Posters.dot

Fractions Graphing.xlt

Graph Paper.xlt

Hangman.xlt

Homework Recordkeeping.xlt

Lab Sheets.dot

Lists and Charts.xlt

Make Your Own Minibook.pot

Newsletter Wizard.wiz

Our Fifty States.pot

Periodic Table.xlt

Polls and Surveys.dot

Recognition Certificates.dot

Schedule.xlt

School Reports.dot

Science Fair Project.pot

Story Map Outline.dot

Student Book Log.xlt

Taking Notes and Outlining.dot

Timeline.xlt

To Do List.xlt

Word Scramble.xlt

Workplace Skills.dot

Writing Checklist.dot

Writing Rubric.dot